SCOTTIE SCHEFFLER

THE INSPIRING STORY OF ONE OF GOLF'S GREATEST CHAMPIONS

JORDAN ANDERS

TABLE OF CONTENTS

Introduction

Golf, for many of us, is more than just a game—it's a pursuit, a passion, and a challenging activity that requires practice and mental focus.

The game is simple in its essence: Hit the ball, find it, and hit it over and over again, until we manage to sink it into that small, distant hole in as few strokes as possible. Yet beneath this apparent simplicity lies a complexity that captivates millions around the world.

Golf is unique in that it offers something for everyone, regardless of age, skill level, or even physical ability. It's a game where we often compete against ourselves, trying to one-up our previous best round. It's a test of patience, strategy, and skill. Each round is a new adventure, with the course itself playing the role of an unpredictable adversary— one moment offering a sense of triumph, the next a humbling lesson in humility, and sometimes even shame. It's this dual nature that makes golf so compelling; the joy of a perfectly struck shot, the camaraderie of playing with friends, and the peaceful activity of playing alone all contribute to the sport's popularity.

Consider the experience of watching your ball soar through the air, perfectly lined up, only gently landing on the green, rolling ever closer to the hole. It's a moment of pure satisfaction, a reward for the hours of practice and the mental focus that the game demands. But even when our shots don't go as planned, when the ball veers off course or stubbornly refuses to sink into the hole, golf teaches us some important lessons. It's about moving forward, shot after shot, maintaining composure, and finding joy in the process rather than just the outcome.

Golf is more than just a sport; it's an experience that combines the beauty of the outdoors with the thrill of a well-played game. It's a game of strategy that allows for personal growth, both physically and mentally, and provides a sense of community among those who love playing it.

Whether you're sharing the day with friends, enjoying a quiet round by yourself, or working to refine your swing at home, golf offers a mix of relaxation and challenge that keeps players coming back, time and time again. This is the essence of golf—a rewarding pursuit that, much like life, is as much about the journey as it is about the destination.

But for some, simply enjoying the sport isn't enough, and obsession leads to an intense competitive spirit. That is, in fact, one of the driving factors behind the career success of Scottie Scheffler, one of today's top golfers. From his early days swinging a club when he was just three years old to becoming the top-ranked golfer in the world, Scottie's ascent has been captivating to watch.

Scottie's list of accomplishments so far has been highly impressive. Since turning professional in 2018, he's rapidly climbed the ranks, amassing 12 PGA Tour victories by 2024. As Scheffler has come to dominate the golf world, he has won major tournaments with levels of poise and precision that have drawn comparisons to the greats of the game.

What makes Scheffler's story so inspiring is not just his success on the course, but the manner in which he has achieved it. Known for his calm demeanor and unshakable focus, Scheffler has become a model of consistency in a sport where the margins between victory and defeat are razor-thin.

His ability to perform under pressure, as seen in his historic run of four wins in five starts in 2024, including the Arnold Palmer Invitational and the Players Championship, shows that his mental game is as refined as his swing. Even though he's achieved remarkable success already, at such a young age, Scottie remains grounded, often attributing his success to his strong faith and the support of his family.

The numbers behind Scheffler's achievements paint a picture of dominance rarely seen in modern golf. In just 51 starts since his first win in 2022, he has secured 10 victories and recorded an astounding 23 top-three finishes. His performance in Strokes Gained: Tee-to-Green, where he has led the PGA Tour by huge margins, has more than proven his technical mastery of the game. These statistics place Scottie in the same class as legends like Tiger Woods, a comparison that is as much a compliment as it is an acknowledgment of the heights he has reached.

As we learn the details of Scottie Scheffler's rise to success, we'll start to unravel the qualities that set him apart: his discipline, his strategic approach to the game, and the humility with which he carries his success.

What could be the secret behind Scheffler's meteoric rise?

It's a question that many golf enthusiasts want to know, but almost nobody can answer. As you turn the pages, you'll uncover the principles and practices that have propelled him to the top of the golfing world.

Whether you're a seasoned golfer yourself or are fairly new to the sport, Scottie's life story is sure to be one of great interest to anyone who's stepped out onto the fairway.

PART I

Scottie's Early Life

CHAPTER 1

Young Scottie Scheffler

Golf, like measles, should be caught young.

–P.G. Wodehouse

Meet the Scheffler Family

Scottie's Mom: Diane

Diane Scheffler née DeLorenzo is more than just Scottie's mom; she has been a driving force behind the financial success of her family and in turn Scottie's amazingly successful career.

A legal industry veteran with over three decades of experience, Diane has consistently balanced the demands of a high-powered career with the equally challenging role of raising a family. Her influence on Scottie's life and his golf career cannot be overstated.

Diane was from Park Ridge, New Jersey, a town known for having a significant Italian-American population, with approximately 17 percent of its residents sharing this heritage (Rahul, 2024). Diane went to Park

Ridge High School, and the late actor James Gandolfini, from the HBO series *The Sopranos*, was one of her classmates.

After graduating from high school, Diane pursued an impressive academic path, earning a B.S. in Economics at Wharton, and later obtaining an M.B.A. in Finance at NYU's Stern School of Business.

Her education led to a successful career in management, where she has held top finance and operations roles at several big national law firms. As of the time of the writing of this book, she currently serves as the Chief Operating Officer at Foley Hoag LLP.

While Diane's professional achievements are noteworthy, it's been her role as the matriarch of the Scheffler family that truly defines her. When the family relocated from New Jersey to Texas in the wake of the 9/11 terrorist attacks, it was Diane's new job that prompted the move.

Despite her demanding career, Diane has always put family first. She has been a constant source of support and inspiration for Scottie, balancing her professional life with her responsibilities as a mother.

Scottie's Dad: Scott Sr.

Scott Scheffler Sr. has been more than just a supportive father to Scottie; he has been the guiding light throughout Scottie's journey to becoming one of the world's top golfers.

From the earliest days, Scott Sr. was the one holding the flashlight as young Scottie practiced his swing late into the night at the modest Orchard Hills Golf Course in New Jersey. This wasn't just a father indulging his son's hobby; it was the beginning of a lifelong bond built around a shared passion for golf.

Scott Sr., who, like Diane, also grew up in New Jersey, played an important role in shaping Scottie's early life and character. Scott Sr. was one of five siblings, raised in the town of Englewood Cliffs, New Jersey, where his dad worked as a car salesman.

Despite the suburban wealth around them, and Englewood Cliffs' proximity to the glitz and glam of Manhattan, the Schefflers lived modestly. Instead of going to fancy country clubs, Scott and his brother Peter would join their father for rounds of golf at the public Overpeck course in nearby Teaneck. Scott Sr. is quick to admit that he was never too good at golf himself, though he did love playing with his dad and brother. His son Scottie would inherit both the passion and the talent.

Unlike many families, where the mother often assumes the role of primary caregiver, the Scheffler family dynamic was different. With Diane, Scottie's mother, working long hours in a demanding legal career, Scott Sr. became the stay-at-home dad, taking charge of the day-to-day responsibilities of raising Scottie and his three sisters. This arrangement gave Scottie the foundation of support he needed to pursue his golf dreams.

The family's move from New Jersey to Dallas, Texas, when Scottie was just six marked a big turning point in Scottie's golfing journey. Yet despite the geographical shift, Scott Sr. ensured that the values and roots they established in New Jersey were never lost. He was the steady presence at Scottie's side, from those early days in New Jersey all the way to the heights of the Masters in Augusta.

Scott Sr.'s influence on Scottie went way beyond just encouragement and logistical support. He instilled in his son a deep sense of humility and balance, ensuring that Scottie remained grounded no matter how high his achievements in golf took him. This is exemplified by the words Scott Sr. shared with his son after his victory at the WGC-Match Play in 2022: "I'm more proud of who you are than your golf" (Politi, 2022).

Their relationship was on full display during Scottie's triumphant 2022 Masters win. As Scottie navigated the pressure of the final round, it was Scott Sr. who, despite his own nerves, provided the steady support that Scottie needed. When Scottie struggled emotionally before the final round, it was the love and assurance from his father, along with the rest of his family, that helped him regain his focus. Scott Sr.'s pride was evident as he watched his son don the green jacket, a moment that was the culmination of years of dedication, sacrifice, and a deep father-son bond.

Scottie's Sisters: Callie, Sara, and Mollie

Throughout his life, Scottie was surrounded by a trio of supportive and competitive sisters—Callie, Sara, and Mollie. His three sisters have shared in his love for sports, and have each played their own roles in shaping the person and athlete he is today.

As the eldest of the Scheffler siblings, Callie naturally assumed the role of protector and guide for her younger brother, Scottie. Born in 1994, she was just two years older than Scottie, but those two years gave her the maturity to help guide him through the early stages of his golfing career.

Callie's involvement in golf was more than just casual; she golfed in the college team at Texas A&M. Her passion for the game and her brother's success was evident when she took on the role of his caddie during the 2016 U.S. Open, where Scottie competed as an amateur. This experience helped strengthen their sibling bond while showing Callie's deep understanding of the game and her unwavering support for Scottie.

Despite her own accomplishments, Callie's pride in her brother has always been paramount. Her role wasn't limited to just carrying his clubs; she provided emotional support and a calming presence during the intense moments of competition. This bond was highlighted when Scottie, as a Masters champion, invited Callie to play a round at Augusta National—a rare privilege he earned by winning the prestigious tournament. Callie, who had no idea about the surprise, was deeply touched and relished the opportunity to share such a special moment with her brother, attesting to their close relationship.

Sara, Scottie's middle sister, may not have had as much time in the spotlight as Callie, but her influence on Scottie is equally important. A graduate of the University of Texas at Austin who studied finance and sustainability, Sara also dabbled in golf during her collegiate years. While she didn't pursue the sport as competitively as Scottie, her involvement in golf and other sports contributed to the competitive atmosphere within the Scheffler household.

Sara's calm demeanor and steady presence have always provided a counterbalance to the high-stakes world of professional golf. During tournaments, especially in moments of high tension, Sara has been there for Scottie, offering her brother quiet but steadfast support. Scottie has often acknowledged the importance of his family's presence during his tournaments, and Sara's role, though less visible, has been vital in helping him maintain focus and composure.

Mollie, Scottie's youngest sister, might have had the least experience in the competitive golfing world, but her impact on Scottie's life is no less significant. A graduate of Texas A&M with a degree in psychology, Mollie's academic pursuits point to a deep understanding of human behavior, something that has undoubtedly influenced her interactions with her brother. Her background in psychology has likely provided her with tools to offer Scottie emotional and mental support, which is crucial in a sport as mentally demanding as golf.

Mollie's contribution to Scottie's success often comes in the form of emotional grounding. As Scottie navigates the pressures of being one of the world's top golfers, having a sister who understands the psychological aspects of performance and stress is invaluable. Mollie, along with her other sisters, has always been there to remind Scottie of the importance of family, providing a grounding influence when the pressures of the professional world are just too much.

Growing up in a competitive environment with three sisters, Scottie was never alone in his pursuits. Whether it was Callie caddying for him, Sara quietly supporting him from the sidelines, or Mollie offering psychological insights, Scottie's sisters have been integral to his success. They have been there for the highs, like his Masters victories, and the lows, providing a support system that has kept Scottie grounded and focused on what truly matters.

Scottie's bond with his sisters shows how the power of the Scheffler family is deeply rooted not in just the high earning power of the matriarch Diane, but in love and mutual respect, showing us that behind every great athlete is a team of supporters who helped them get there.

New Jersey

Scottie's early years were spent in Ridgewood, New Jersey, a suburban village in Bergen County known for its affluence and proximity to New York City. With tree-lined streets and historic homes, Ridgewood offered the Scheffler family a comfortable lifestyle that many would envy. The town's high-ranking public schools and pricey private academies, manicured parks, and proximity to cultural hubs provided Scottie and his siblings with access to a wealth of opportunities.

Growing up in such a privileged environment undoubtedly had an influence on Scottie's early years. Despite this idyllic setting though, Ridgewood's proximity to the crime-ridden streets of New York City also meant the harsh realities of the world were just a short car ride away.

This became even more clear with the terrorist attacks on September 11, 2001, an event that profoundly impacted the Scheffler family, as they did many others in the region. The attacks, which happened just around 25 miles or so from their home, instilled a deep sense of vulnerability and fear in the community.

It's possible that it was this growing fear, coupled with a desire for a safer, more secure environment, that ultimately prompted the Schefflers to leave their comfortable life in New Jersey and relocate to Dallas, Texas. Diane's new job offer, however, was of course the primary motivating factor. The move to Texas marked a big shift in the Scheffler family's life. Dallas, a city known for its deep-rooted conservative values, was a far cry from the liberal, cosmopolitan atmosphere of Ridgewood, which is nestled in the heart of traditionally Blue Bergen County.

The Schefflers' decision to move to a southern red state may have been influenced by more than just concerns about safety. It suggests a possible alignment with the values and political ideologies that are prevalent in Texas, a state known for its emphasis on individual freedoms.

In Texas, the Schefflers found a new home, but also possibly a place that resonated with their evolving worldview. The transition from the more secular, liberal-leaning environment of Ridgewood to the more religious, conservative landscape of Texas likely played a role in shaping Scottie's identity as he grew into a young man and a professional golfer.

Scottie fully embraced the Texan way of life, from his demeanor to his choice to study at the University of Texas in Austin. This shift is evident in how he carries himself on and off the golf course, embodying the cavalier confidence and independence often associated with the Lone Star state. That said, as reported by his wife Meredith, "When people say he was born and raised in Texas, he'll be the first one to say, 'No, I was born in New Jersey'" (O'Connor, 2021).

While Scottie's time in New Jersey was brief, the town remains an important part of his family's story. Even as he embraced his new life in Texas, the memories of his early years in New Jersey—hitting golf balls in his backyard in Bergen County—provided a foundation for his golf career. As much as Scottie identifies with his Texas roots today, there's no denying that the shadows of Ridgewood and the experiences of his early childhood helped mold the man he would become.

Scottie's Roots and Religion

While Diane's ancestry is Italian-American, from his father's side, Scottie inherits German ancestry. Today, Scottie's connection to his Italian heritage is reflected in his family's devout Roman Catholic faith. This faith was evident in his marriage to his high school sweetheart, Meredith Scudder, which was celebrated in a traditional religious ceremony.

His Childhood and Introduction to Golf

Scott Sr. was totally committed to his four kids. One of the most important activities he did with Scottie and his sisters was their frequent trips to the Bergen Community College golf course in Paramus, New Jersey.

Golfing by Flashlight

Evenings at the golf course became a regular occurrence, where Scottie, then just a young boy, practiced his swings under the dimming light, with Scott Sr. holding a flashlight to light up the green.

These nighttime practice sessions were more than just for fun; they became foundational experiences that contributed significantly to

Scottie's development as a golfer. Despite the informal setting, these shared moments provided Scottie with early exposure to a real golf course environment, with the added challenge of it being dark outside. This helped him develop his skills while building a deep love for the game.

While not all of Scottie's sisters may have pursued golf as fervently as he did, these outings were a family affair, again showing the close-knit nature of the Scheffler family and their collective support for Scottie's growing passion.

The importance of these early experiences of golfing by flashlight cannot be overstated. They laid a strong roadmap in place for Scottie and his sisters' future success in life and in sports. Scott Sr. was instrumental in helping his kids build discipline and endurance against all kinds of obstacles and challenges they came to face.

Scott Sr.'s nighttime visits to Bergen Community College with his kids in tow have come to symbolize the humble beginnings of a future Masters champion, a journey that started on the modest greens of a local college course in New Jersey, guided by the strong, highly involved support of a dedicated father.

The Scheffler kids loved practicing putting with their dad at the community college course, but one day, Scott Sr. decided they were finally ready to try out an even better one! Orchard Hills Golf Course is a modest nine-hole course that's right near some of New Jersey's more prestigious clubs. It's a place that came to hold a special place in Scottie's early golfing story.

Orchard Hills

Recognizable by its weathered green clubhouse, Orchard Hills is far from the grandeur of Augusta National. But it was here that a young Scottie, barely old enough to grip a club, began to take his game seriously. Scott Sr. would bring Scottie and the girls to the course regularly. Sometimes Scottie's oldest sister Callie would be busy training at the nearby Bergen Community College pool, where she excelled at swimming.

As he had done over at the community college course, Scott Sr. would illuminate the course with a flashlight as Scottie practiced in the dim evening light. Though practicing at twilight meant that sometimes Scott Sr. would get hit by errant golf balls, some of which even left him with severe bruising, he didn't care. Nothing could deter him from helping his son pursue his passion as best as he could.

While the superintendent at the course, Pete Evans, doesn't even remember meeting young Scottie today, he has proudly acknowledged the course's role in the making of a legend, characterizing Scottie's success, which all started with his training at Orchard Hills, as being a great piece of New Jersey lore (Politi, 2023).

As Scottie took his first swings at courses like Orchard Hills, Scott Sr. could hardly have imagined that these modest beginnings would lead to a future where his son would stand among the golfing elite. The dedication to the sport that Scottie exhibited as a young child, under the watchful eye of his father, helped him build a sense of stability and security, and also the mental toughness and skill that would eventually earn him the green jacket at the Masters.

A Big Move

The Scheffler family's move from New Jersey to Texas marked a big turning point in Scottie's life. Diane had accepted the position of Chief Operating Officer at Thompson & Knight LLP. The decision to uproot their lives from the familiar surroundings of northern New Jersey was not taken lightly, particularly with four young children in tow, but it was a move that would have an outsized impact on Scottie's future.

Before the move to Dallas, Diane had worked tirelessly to establish herself as an influential figure in the legal profession. She had already spent time as a business manager for the Executive Committee at Skadden, where she honed her skills in organizational leadership and strategic planning over 13 years. Her experience, coupled with her earlier experience in IT and consulting at Merrill Lynch and Arthur Young, equipped her with a broad understanding of the complexities of the overall picture of law firm operations.

As COO of Thompson & Knight LLP, Diane was responsible for providing strategic direction and overseeing the firm's operations, including finance, human resources, IT, and marketing. Her leadership helped boost the firm's profitability and helped it stay competitive.

Diane's role at the prestigious AM 100 firm wasn't just any old job; it was a chance for her to make an impact. Her work there was characterized by a focus on innovation and efficiency, anticipating clients' needs, and delivering cost-effective solutions, all of which were critical in the highly competitive and ruthless environment of corporate law.

Upon their arrival in Dallas, the Scheffler family quickly acclimated to their new environment. It was a place of tall buildings and big cowboy hats where the wealthy liked to flaunt all that they had. They decided that Diane's sky-high salary warranted the family joining the exclusive Royal Oaks Country Club. This decision proved to be pivotal, as it was here that Scottie met a man named Randy Smith, the storied golf swing coach who would continue to guide him throughout his career. Smith's mentorship, combined with the club's top-notch facilities, provided the then six-year-old Scottie with the resources and support he needed to elevate his game.

The move to Texas was a big change for everyone, but it also served to reinforce the family's unique dynamic. Diane and Scott Sr. knew that they had to pay extra special attention to the needs of their children. With Diane's demanding but highly lucrative job seeing the family reach new heights economically, Scott would continue to dedicate his life to the care and support of Scottie and his three sisters. This arrangement allowed Diane to pursue her career while making sure that Scottie and his sisters would have all the attention and encouragement they needed to thrive, both in their personal lives and in their various activities, including Scottie's burgeoning golf career.

Reflecting on the impact of his family's big move to Texas, today, Scottie remains well aware of the risks his parents took and the sacrifices they made for him and his sisters. He often speaks of the strong bond he shares with both his parents, and has been open about the important role his father played in nurturing his athletic talents, and also the contributions of his mother in supporting the family financially and emotionally. The relocation to Texas, though challenging at first, ultimately provided Scottie with opportunities that may not have been available had the family remained in New Jersey.

Don't Forget!

- Born in New Jersey, Scottie may be a Texas star, but he's still proud of his Garden State origins.
- Scottie's dad, Scott Sr., would light up the night with a flashlight so young Scottie could practice his swing—talk about dedication!
- The Scheffler family swapped a view of the NYC skyline for the big Texas sky after 9/11, and Scottie traded modest New Jersey courses for fancy Dallas greens.

- From caddying sisters to a stay-at-home dad, Scottie's success is a full-family affair. The Schefflers are proof that teamwork, family, and faith make the dream work!

Did You Know?

- Scottie's lucky number is 13!
- He carries a lucky bicentennial quarter from 1976 in his pocket at every match.
- Scottie was into basketball as a kid, and he still enjoys the occasional pick-up game.

Up Next

Now that we've learned about Scottie's formative years and his family's big move, it's time to explore the next phase of his life—his high school and college years. These were the years when Scottie began to truly amp up his skills, as he faced his first real competition.

In the next chapter, we'll follow Scottie through the highs and lows of his teenage years, the moments that tested his resolve, and the experiences that pushed him ever closer to achieving his golf dreams.

CHAPTER 2

❦

The Path to The PGA Tour

A bad attitude is worse than a bad swing.

–Payne Stewart

Scottie's School Days

Growing up, Scottie wasn't just a golf prodigy; he was an all-around athlete and loved all different sports, including basketball and table tennis.

Scottie became known for his fluid and effortless style on the basketball court. Standing at 6' 3", he had a natural athleticism that made him a pretty good player. Despite being obsessed with golf, Scottie never gave up his passion for basketball. He enjoyed the camaraderie and the break it provided from the intense discipline of golf.

Scottie's high school basketball coach was impressed by how easily he could switch from being a top golfer to a key player on the basketball team. His ability to dunk, combined with his strategic thinking and hand-eye coordination, made him a standout on the court. These same skills translated seamlessly into his golf game, where his physical fitness and mental agility set him apart from his peers.

Table tennis was another sport where Scottie's competitive spirit shone through. Known for his intense focus and sharp reflexes, he'd often challenge friends to friendly yet fiercely competitive matches during high school. His quick reflexes and precise hand-eye coordination, honed through countless hours of table tennis, became invaluable assets in his golfing career. Whether it was a high-stakes golf tournament or a casual game, Scottie approached every challenge with the same intensity and drive to win

Even as he transitioned into professional golf, Scottie continued to play these other sports, albeit more cautiously to avoid injury. Having other athletic interests besides golf has kept him physically fit while providing him with a mental edge.

Randy Smith: Scheffler's Golf Coach

During his high school days, Scottie came to be deeply influenced by his relationship with Randy Smith, a legendary golf coach based at Royal Oaks. Smith who has been a mentor to numerous PGA Tour players, including Justin Leonard and Ryan Palmer, first met Scheffler when he was just a kid, when his family had just moved there and became members of the club. It didn't take long for Smith to recognize the raw talent and potential in Scheffler.

Randy Smith is no ordinary golf instructor. Inducted into the PGA of America Hall of Fame in 2005, he's known for his ability to cultivate natural talent from a young age, turning promising junior golfers into accomplished professionals over years of intensive training. His approach to coaching is centered around developing a player's instincts and creativity, rather than imposing a rigid technique. This philosophy played a crucial role in how Scottie's game was shaped.

Scottie started training under Smith's guidance at Royal Oaks when he was just seven years old. What started as a routine 10-minute lesson quickly turned into an hour-and-a-half session, as Smith had no problem spotting the exceptional talent of this young kid who had just moved from New Jersey. Over the years, their relationship grew, with Smith providing the mentorship and expertise that would guide Scottie through the ranks of junior golf and into the amateur and professional circuits.

Smith's coaching style is unique in that he emphasizes the importance of making golf fun and engaging, especially for very young golfers, like Scottie was at the time. Randy's technique focuses on developing kids' natural instincts and encouraging them to be creative with their shots.

Rather than drilling a specific swing technique, for instance, Randy will often ask a younger golfer to figure out how to hit a ball high or low, forcing them to think critically about their strategy and find the answers on their own. Instead of instructing, he'd simply coach and encourage. All Randy had to do was guide Scottie to help find out what worked for him, and his God-given physiology and swing.

This innovative training method worked wonders for Scottie, and he thrived under Smith's tutelage. Randy helped Scottie harness his natural athleticism, making him into a golfer with a distinct and effective style.

As Scottie grew older and his skills sharpened, Randy remained a constant presence in his life, guiding him through the challenges of competitive golf, whether it was refining his grip or working on his mental approach.

The long-standing relationship that was built between coach and student was one founded upon mutual respect and a shared passion for the game, laying the foundation for Scheffler's successes in high school golf and in junior-level amateur competition.

High School Golf and Junior Tournaments

While he had serious skills on the basketball court, Scottie's golfing at Highland Park High School was exceptional. Following in the footsteps of another local golf prodigy, Jordan Spieth, Scottie quickly made a name for himself as one of the top young golfers in the state. Between 2012 and 2014, he managed to clinch three consecutive individual state titles, a record that got him attention as a rising star in the golf world.

These high school titles were crucial in building Scottie's confidence. The consistency he demonstrated during these years was the result of his dedication to training with Randy since he was seven, and a level of discipline that was highly commendable. Scottie's success at Highland Park was more than just a stepping stone; it marked the beginning of a new chapter in the making of a future PGA Tour star.

While Scottie's high school achievements were impressive, his performances in American Junior Golf Association (AJGA) events allowed him to further flex his true potential. Competing against the best junior golfers in the entire country, he held his own against other talented young golfers and often emerged victorious. His success in these events was an indicator of his ability to compete at the highest levels of junior golf.

One of the most notable achievements of Scottie's junior career was being named the 2013 Rolex Junior Player of the Year, a prestigious honor awarded by the AJGA to the most outstanding junior golfers of the year. This placed Scottie in the company of golf legends like Tiger Woods, Phil Mickelson, and Jordan Spieth, all of whom had previously won the award as juniors.

Scottie's participation in events like the Polo Golf Junior Classic and his consistently high finishes in AJGA tournaments proved his ability to perform under pressure and against the toughest competition. These experiences were invaluable in preparing him for the challenges of collegiate and professional golf.

Throughout his junior career, Scottie consistently finished in the top ranks of tournaments, but not every appearance was a screaming success. At just 16 years old, Scottie was already showing flashes of brilliance that hinted at his future potential. However, as with any young golfer, there were tough lessons to be learned—especially in the high-stakes world of match play.

During the 2012 U.S. Junior Amateur Championship, Scottie experienced firsthand the unpredictable nature of the format. Coming off a string of impressive performances, including a 10-under 61 at Northwood Club that broke the course record, he entered the tournament with high expectations. His first-round match seemed to justify those expectations, as he steamrolled his opponent, Brandon Bauman, in a dominant 7 and 6 victory.

However, the game of golf has a way of humbling even the most talented players. In the Round of 32, Scottie faced Tae Wan Lee of Korea in a match that would test his mental toughness and ability to handle pressure. Despite taking an early lead, he found himself in a see-saw battle that showcased the volatile nature of match play. After a series of missed putts and a few unlucky breaks, Scottie was two down with just a few holes to play.

Even though he fought back, cutting the deficit and nearly turning the tide, Lee's consistent play and a clutch birdie on the 16th hole ultimately sealed Scottie's fate. It was a bitter pill to swallow, especially given how well he had played throughout the match. After the game, Scottie acknowledged that Lee was just too tough to defeat.

This early exit in the 2012 U.S. Junior Amateur Championship was a tough lesson in the complexities of match play. It was a reminder that in golf, no lead is ever truly safe, and every shot counts—especially when you're up against a competitor playing their best. For Scottie, it was another step in his journey, one that would prepare him for success the next year.

The 2013 U.S. Junior Amateur Championship

Held at the challenging Martis Camp Club in Truckee, California, the 2013 Junior Amateur Championship saw Scottie demonstrating his high level of technical skill and mental toughness as he claimed one of the most prestigious titles in junior golf.

Entering the championship as the third seed after a strong performance in stroke-play qualifying, Scottie's climb to the top of the rankings was anything but easy. He faced stiff competition from some of the best junior golfers in the country. It was in the final match against Davis Riley that he showed what he was truly made of.

The match against Riley was a 36-hole battle, and for much of it, Scottie found himself trailing. At one point, he was two holes down with just nine to play. He had to dig deep to muster up the energy he needed, and he powered through. From that point onward, there was no stopping him as he raced to the finish line.

By the 28th hole, Scottie had mounted an impressive comeback. He capitalized on a missed par putt by Riley on the 13th hole, which evened the match and shifted the momentum in Scottie's favor. From there, he birdied the 14th hole to take his first lead of the match, and he never looked back. By the 34th hole, Scottie had secured a 3-and-2 victory, capping off his final appearance as a junior golfer with the ultimate prize.

This victory was significant for several reasons. It made Scottie the sixth Texan to win the U.S. Junior Amateur since 1999, placing him in the company of greats like Hunter Mahan and Jordan Spieth (*Scheffler Defeats Riley to Win U.S. Junior Amateur*, 2013). The big win put him in the top 20 of the World Amateur Golf Ranking, making him one of the best golfers in the entire world, despite still being a teenager!

Coach Randy Smith was moved to tears watching Scottie's big win.

The Junior Invitational at Sage Valley

The next year, Scottie pulled off another impressive win. He entered the final round of the Junior Invitational with a one-shot lead over Theo Humphrey, a tough opponent who was headed to Vanderbilt. However, it was Cameron Champ, another highly touted junior and a future star on the PGA Tour, who provided the most intense competition as the round progressed. Champ's late-round surge, highlighted by a birdie and eagle on consecutive holes, put immense pressure on Scottie as they approached the closing stretch of the tournament.

Despite the mounting pressure, Scottie showed poise and composure. He had already set the tone for his round with three consecutive birdies on the front nine and added two more birdies on the back nine, including crucial ones on the 13th and 15th holes. As the tournament came down to the wire, Scottie and Champ found themselves tied with just three holes to play.

It was on the 18th hole where Scottie's calm demeanor and intense level of focus made all the difference. While Champ struggled to a bogey, Scottie was able to safely navigate the hole, securing a par to clinch the victory by a single stroke. This triumph at Sage Valley was more than just another win; it was a defining moment that again confirmed Scheffler's status as the top junior golfer in the United States.

By this time, Scottie's consistent performances and ability to prevail in high-stakes situations had propelled him to the upper echelons of junior golf, earning him widespread praise and much-warranted recognition as the nation's best junior golfer. This period marked the beginning of a trajectory that would see him transition seamlessly into a successful PGA debut as an amateur.

Scottie's PGA Tour Debut

At just 17 years old, Scottie Scheffler made a huge splash in the golfing world by making the cut at the 2014 HP Byron Nelson Championship, giving him his first appearance in a PGA Tour event.

Scottie entered the tournament as the youngest participating golfer, fresh off his third consecutive state title at the UIL tournament in Austin. Despite his young age, he approached the tournament with the poise and confidence of a pro. He was put to the test during the first two rounds, and delivered, posting scores of 71 and 68, respectively, to finish at 1-under par and secure his place for the weekend rounds.

The highlight of his second round came on the par-3 17th hole, where Scottie rolled in a 34-foot birdie putt, eliciting a roar from the gallery. His strong finish, including a steady par on the 18th hole, ensured he would make the cut, an accomplishment that placed him among the top 41 golfers in the tournament at that point.

Making the cut in his PGA Tour debut was no small feat, especially considering the challenges he had faced on the course. He navigated some tough situations, including recovering from a poor drive on the first hole of his second round by saving par, showing that all the strategic thinking skills Randy Smith helped him develop had more than paid off.

Despite having made the cut, Scottie's ambitions extended way beyond just participating in the tournament. He had entered with a goal to finish in the top 10, a mindset that speaks volumes about his competitive nature. Although he momentarily achieved a position within the top 10 during the early stages of the second round, he ended up finishing tied in 22nd place.

Though he didn't achieve his top-10 goal during his first PGA appearance, this awesome debut performance placed Scheffler in the same class as other young prodigies like fellow Texan Jordan Spieth, who had already made a similar impact at the Byron Nelson Championship four years earlier. The comparisons between Scheffler and Spieth were inevitable, given their similar paths through junior golf in Dallas and their shared achievements, including both winning the U.S. Junior Amateur Championship.

Scheffler's performance at the Byron Nelson Championship not only demonstrated his raw talent in front of a large audience; it also provided him with invaluable experience competing against professionals. As an amateur participating in the tournament, he was unfortunately not eligible for the $60,000 payout that would have accompanied his performance if he had already been pro.

Don't Forget!

- Coached by PGA Hall of Famer Randy Smith since the age of seven, Scottie's swing has always been in good hands—or should we say, legendary ones.
- In the 2012 U.S. Junior Amateur, Scottie learned that golf can be as unpredictable as a Texas weather forecast—tough losses build tougher champions.

- Named 2013 Rolex Junior Player of the Year, Scottie joined the ranks of Tiger Woods and Phil Mickelson like it was nothing!
- Scottie won the 2013 U.S. Junior Amateur Championship in epic comeback fashion, solidifying his place among the greats.
- Meanwhile, at the Texas State high school level, Scottie snagged three consecutive state golf titles from 2012 to 2014. Take that, Jordan Spieth!

Did You Know?

- Scottie is super afraid of heights.
- He loves the TV show *The Office,* and his favorite character is Dwight Schrute.
- Scottie has said that fellow Ryder-cup golfers Doug Ghim and Bryson DeChambeau are fun to play table tennis against and that they're actually pretty good, though maybe not as good as him!

Up Next

As impressive as Scottie's achievements as a junior golfer were, they were just the beginning. The next chapter will take us deeper into Scottie's journey as he transitions from amateur phenom to college golf standout at the University of Texas, where he faced new challenges, sharpened his skills, and began eyeing the ultimate goal: going pro!

PART II

The Rise of a Golf Superstar

CHAPTER 3

Scottie's Early Success

*I can hold my head high... I did my best out there
today and fought hard.*

–Scottie Scheffler

Scottie's College Career: Golf at the University of Texas

After high school, Scottie went off to Austin to play golf at the University of Texas for the Longhorns. Once there, he quickly established himself as a standout player, bringing his high school momentum into one of the most prestigious college golf programs in the whole country.

As a freshman in 2014, Scottie was already a decorated junior golfer, and he wasted no time making an impact at the collegiate level. Under the guidance of head coach John Fields, Scottie flourished, becoming a key contributor to the team. Well-respected by his peers for his calm demeanor and relentless work ethic, he continued delivering strong performances, helping the Longhorns remain a dominant force in NCAA golf.

He claimed back-to-back victories at the Western Intercollegiate and the Big 12 Championship, proving his ability to compete and win against some of the best collegiate golfers in the country. His victory at the Western Intercollegiate was equally impressive, as he defeated seven of the top 25 players in the nation.

The 2015 Big 12

Competing at the prestigious Southern Hills Country Club, Scottie showed composure and skill beyond his years at the 2015 Big 12, finishing the tournament with a score of even-par 280. This achievement marked him as the fifth player in Texas Men's Golf history to earn this honor, and it was his second consecutive win after a victory at the Western Intercollegiate earlier that month (Persac, 2015).

The Longhorns' team performance was equally impressive, as they clinched their third straight Big 12 Championship title, finishing 24 strokes ahead of Texas Tech. This dominant victory also set a new Big 12 record for the margin of victory at a championship, pointing to the team's exceptional talent and cohesion (Persac, 2015).

Scottie's victory was particularly noteworthy given the challenging conditions of the Southern Hills course, which demanded precision and accuracy from the tee and fairway. His rounds of 72, 67, 68, and 73 highlighted his consistency and ability to perform under pressure. Despite a rough start in the final round, Scottie managed to turn things around, contributing to the Longhorns' overall success.

This strong showing at the Big 12 Championship further solidified his reputation as a rising star in collegiate golf and provided the Longhorns with momentum heading into the NCAA Regionals.

Receiving the Phil Mickelson Freshman of the Year Award

After what was a stellar freshman year, Scottie was named the recipient of the Phil Mickelson Freshman of the Year award for his excellent performance. One of the most prestigious honors in collegiate golf, the award is given annually to the most outstanding freshman in Division I men's golf.

Named after the legendary golfer Phil Mickelson, who himself made a big impact as a college golfer before turning professional, the award recognizes a player who has demonstrated exceptional talent, performance, and potential during their first year of college competition.

Throughout the rest of his college career, Scottie's game continued to mature. His time at Texas saw him compete in numerous high-pressure tournaments, where he continued to perform at a high level. He was instrumental in leading the Longhorns to multiple Big 12 Championships, showing that he was great in individual competition and also as part of a team. Scottie's contributions weren't just limited to his play on the course; he also emerged as a leader among his peers, respected for his discipline and commitment to the sport.

In addition to his team achievements, Scottie's individual awards at the college level began to pile up. He earned All-American honors multiple times, flexing his skills against the top collegiate golfers in the nation.

The 2016 Big 12

In 2016, Scottie Scheffler helped the Longhorns continue their dominance in collegiate golf by helping them secure their fourth consecutive Big 12 Championship title at Whispering Pines Golf Club in Trinity, Texas. Already ranked number one nationally, the Longhorns ended up setting a new Big 12 Championship record with a total score of 1,135, finishing 26 strokes ahead of their nearest competitor, Oklahoma State.

Although Scottie didn't repeat as the individual champion this year, his contributions still boosted the team's success. He finished in ninth place overall with an even-par score of 288, highlighted by a final-round 68. This helped the Longhorns establish a commanding lead on the final day of the tournament.

Scottie's efforts were part of a broader team success, with several of his teammates also finishing in the top 10. Beau Hossler tied for second place, ping-pong pal Doug Ghim finished fourth, and Gavin Hall tied for sixth, showing the depth of talent on the Texas roster. The team's final round was especially impressive, with four players shooting subpar rounds to break multiple Big 12 Championship records, including the most subpar rounds in a single championship.

Scottie's Academic Merits

Scottie's success went way beyond the golf course during his time at UT. While he was making headlines as a key player on the university's top-ranked golf team, Scottie was also achieving academic praise.

As a finance major, he was named to the 2016 Academic All-Big 12 First Team, a recognition reserved for students who maintain a GPA between 3.2 and 4.0. This achievement proved his ability to balance the demanding schedule of a top-tier student athlete, excelling in his studies and on the golf course.

The 2016 U.S. Open
The Qualifier

In 2016, Scottie was well on his way to his first U.S. Open appearance. The long road to the tournament began with an impressive performance during the sectional qualifying round in Columbus, Ohio. Just 19 years old and fresh off helping the University of Texas to the NCAA Championship finals, Scheffler showed both his talent and composure under pressure during this high-stakes event.

The qualifier had many weather delays and unusual circumstances that year, including a near-darkness finish that tested the nerves of even the most seasoned players, even ones like Scottie, who had learned to play golf in the dark with his dad holding that old trusty flashlight. Scottie managed to navigate the weather and darkness challenges with skill.

Playing without any partners for the last part of his round due to withdrawals, Scottie managed to stay focused and complete his 36 holes with a score that landed him in a playoff round for a spot in the U.S. Open. The match was nerve-wracking, but Scottie clinched his place in the prestigious tournament with a crucial par save on the final hole.

The Tournament

Arriving at Oakmont Country Club, Scottie was about to face one of the toughest tests in golf. But the young Texan proved he was ready for the challenge. In the first round, Scottie shot an impressive 1-under par 69, putting him briefly in the clubhouse lead as weather conditions once again played a role, causing several delays throughout the day. Despite the interruptions, his steady play, including three birdies and solid lag putting, kept him in contention.

Scottie's success that first day was all the more notable considering the external distractions. With his older sister Callie serving as his caddie—a role she had taken on in several tournaments before—Scottie managed to keep his nerves in check, focusing on his game rather than the massive scale of the event. His mental toughness was on full display, as he skillfully adjusted to the changing course conditions caused by the rain, which made controlling the spin on approach shots particularly challenging.

However the second round at Oakmont would not be as kind to Scottie. He struggled to replicate his strong start, shooting a 78 that ultimately led to him missing the cut by just one stroke. Despite the disappointment of not advancing further, Scottie's performance in his first U.S. Open was a clear signal of his potential as a pro.

The 2017 Big 12

In 2017, Scottie and the Texas Longhorns faced one of their toughest challenges yet at the Big 12, which was held at Prairie Dunes Country Club in Hutchinson, Kansas that year. The winds were blowing that year, and it made scoring difficult. Despite this, the Longhorns still were able to get their fifth consecutive Big 12 title.

Scottie played an important team role throughout the championship, starting the final round tied for the individual lead. He had consistently strong performances over the first three rounds, with scores of 77, 70, and 68, showing his ability to adapt to difficult conditions. On the final day, Scottie shot a 73, which left him just short of winning the individual title, as Kansas' Chase Hanna edged him out by a single stroke to take the medalist honors.

Despite the narrow miss for the individual championship, Scottie's performance was crucial for Texas. His steady play, including a clutch putt on the 18th green, helped Texas overcome a six-shot deficit during the final round. The team's collective effort on the last two holes, where they combined to shoot 5-under par, was enough to secure a one-stroke victory over Oklahoma State. This victory marked Texas' first team win of the spring season and extended their dominance in the Big 12.

Scottie's strong showing, alongside his teammates Doug Ghim and Steven Chervony, who also finished in the top 10, showed the depth and range of talent on the Texas squad.

The 2017 U.S. Open

In 2017, at the U.S. Open, which took place at Erin Hills in Wisconsin, Scottie's game was strong from the outset. In the first round, he shot a 3-under 69, placing him among the top amateurs in the tournament, lending him a solid base for success. His consistent playing was a reflection of the confidence he had built throughout his junior season at the University of Texas, where he had notched four straight top-3 finishes leading up to the U.S. Open. This time, Scottie felt more comfortable and assured on the big stage, drawing from his previous year's experience to navigate the challenges of a major championship with greater ease.

Scottie's strong start continued into the second round, and by the end of the day, he had made the cut—an accomplishment in itself for any amateur. Alongside him was Cameron Champ, whom Scottie knew well, as the two had faced off against each other since they were teenagers. Both Scheffler and Champ proved they could hold their own against the world's best golfers, with Champ even climbing into the top 10 during the early rounds.

The final rounds at Erin Hills tested Scottie's endurance and focus. While he couldn't maintain the blistering pace he set on the first day, he still managed to finish the tournament as the low amateur, securing a tie for 27th place with a total score of 1-under par. This achievement placed Scheffler in the esteemed company of a few other former Texas Longhorns who had also earned low amateur honors at the U.S. Open, including Ben Crenshaw, Justin Leonard, and Jordan Spieth.

The 2017 Walker Cup

In 2017, Scottie Scheffler was asked to join the U.S. team for the Walker Cup, the most important amateur golf competition in the world. The U.S. team that year, captained by Spider Miller, was a stellar lineup that included future PGA Tour stars like Collin Morikawa, Cameron Champ, and Will Zalatoris. This team, which some consider to be the best in Walker Cup history, dominated the competition, defeating Great Britain & Ireland by an impressive margin of 19-7.

Scheffler played a supporting role in the victory. The team's synergy and individual talents were apparent from the start, and Scottie, alongside his teammates, showed a level of play that would foreshadow their future Ryder Cup victories.

This team victory was a big milestone in Scottie's amateur career, setting the stage for his transition to professional golf and his rise in the ranks as one of the top players in the world.

The 2017 NCAA Championships

Scottie's performance at the 2017 NCAA Golf Championships proved him to be a golfer who could shine, even under high-pressure situations.

Now in his junior year at UT Scottie entered the final round of the championships at Rich Harvest Farms with the individual lead after three consecutive rounds of 4-under 68. His consistency, especially on the course's par 5s, where he recorded no bogeys across three rounds, showed his ability to rise to the occasion when it mattered most.

Scottie's calm and focused demeanor was evident throughout the tournament, a quality that had been honed through years of competing at the highest levels. He had already made a name for himself in 2013 with his U.S. Junior Amateur win and had defeated top college players in numerous events, including the previous year's NCAA final, where he nearly led Texas to a national title.

Despite an uneasy start to the final round, Scottie chugged forward like a freight train pulling out of the station. He navigated the challenging conditions with precision, especially on the back nine, where he managed to maintain his composure and deliver solid pars under pressure. The final round put his technical skills and mental game to the test, as he battled the elements and the pressure of leading one of the most high-profile college golf tournaments.

Scottie ultimately finished the tournament tied for third with a score of 6-under 282. While he fell short of capturing the individual title, his performance helped keep Texas in contention as a team, showing his deep dedication to his teammates and the program. Scottie's showing at the 2017 NCAA Golf Championships was a clear indication of the promising career that lay ahead, both in amateur and professional golf.

The 2018 NCAA Championship

In the opening round of the 2018 NCAA Championship at Karsten Creek Golf Club, Scottie led the Longhorns with an impressive performance.

He was 4-under par through his first 10 holes, placing him tied for fifth on the individual leaderboard and just one stroke behind the leaders.

Tee time was delayed due to bad weather, but Scottie's strong start helped position the Longhorns in fifth place in the team standings before play was suspended due to the sun setting. The late tee start meant they'd have to pick things up the next day. If only they knew how much Scottie had practiced in the dark as a kid with his dad by flashlight, he could have won the whole thing! Unfortunately, playing in the darkness with flashlights is not allowed under NCAA rules. That year, despite an excellent effort from Scottie and the Longhorns, Oklahoma State took home the prize.

Scholar-Athlete of the Year

In 2018, Scottie Scheffler's excellence on and off the golf course was recognized when he was honored at the Texas Athletics Academic Award Banquet with the Big 12 Scholar-Athlete of the Year award. The honor acknowledged his commitment to both academics and athletics.

Throughout the 2017-2018 season, Scottie was a standout performer for the Longhorns, playing in every event and maintaining an impressive stroke average of 70.59 (*Men's Golf's Scheffler Named Big 12 Scholar Athlete*, 2018). His consistency was evident as he shot 17 of his 27 rounds at or under par, including nine rounds in the 60s.

Scottie's Graduation

In 2018, Scottie graduated from UT with a Bachelor's Degree in Finance. Scottie's success in balancing the demands of being a top collegiate athlete while maintaining a strong academic record was commendable.

Throughout his entire college golf career, Scheffler's family had been a constant source of support and encouragement. His parents had nurtured his love for golf from a young age, and of course, were immensely proud of his accomplishments both on and off the course. They had watched him grow from a talented junior golfer into a well-rounded adult, capable of handling the pressures of elite competition and academic challenges.

Graduating from the University of Texas wasn't just a personal achievement for Scheffler; it was a moment of pride for his entire family. They had witnessed the sacrifices he made, the countless hours spent practicing and studying, and the determination that had driven him to succeed in both arenas. As he walked across the stage to receive his diploma, it was a moment that symbolized the end of one journey but also the beginning of another that would take him far into the world of professional golf and beyond.

Don't Forget!

- Scottie was named to the Academic All-Big 12 First Team in 2016, proving he's not just good with a golf club, but did his homework too!
- He helped the Longhorns win multiple Big 12 Championships, making victory a regular part of his college routine.
- Scottie dominated at the 2017 Walker Cup with what some call the greatest team in history.
- He led Texas at the NCAA Championships, almost clinching the individual title in 2017, but finishing a cool third.

Did You Know?

- Many have wondered what Scottie's all-time favorite club is. He's said that he relies upon his trusty 60-degree wedge like no other club in his bag.

Up Next

Now that Scottie had shown the discipline, dedication, and drive that would soon make him a force to be reckoned with in the world of professional golf, he was ready to take on whatever challenges lay ahead.

As he walked off the graduation stage, diploma in hand, he wasn't just closing a chapter—he was opening the door to a whole new world of possibilities. The next stage of his life would see him stepping onto golf's biggest stages, ready to make his mark as a rising star. Up next, we'll follow Scottie's trajectory from a college standout to a pro golf powerhouse. As the stakes were higher, the competition got fiercer, but the victories got even sweeter.

CHAPTER 4

⧂

Rookie Years

*I feel like I'm maturing as a person on the golf course,
which is a good place to be.*

–Scottie Scheffler

The transition from college athlete to professional sports can be challenging for many young athletes. They often face uncertainty and the pressure to perform. For Scottie, this transition marked the beginning of an extraordinary new chapter in his career and personal life. With every swing, every round, and every tournament, he further solidified his place among the elite in the world of golf.

In this chapter, we'll track Scottie's amazing rookie years, a time when he transformed from a promising young talent into a real competitor on the PGA Tour. It's a story of learning, disappointment, and breakthrough moments that allowed him to build tons of experience to help him eventually reach the top. As he navigated the highs and lows of professional golf, Scottie's maturity on the course became evident, and his dedication to his craft never wavered.

From being named Player of the Year during the 2019 Korn Ferry Tour, to becoming PGA Tour Rookie of the Year in 2020, to finally making an international splash at the Ryder Cup in 2021, we'll look at the key milestones that defined Scottie's rookie years. As we'll see, his tale is of ambition, determination, and the unwavering belief that with enough hard work and the right mindset, anything is possible.

The 2019 Web.com / Korn Ferry Tour
Qualifying for the Event

Scottie earned his Web.com Tour card in 2019 for his standout performances during the qualifying stages. His efforts in obtaining the tour card began the previous year.

In December 2018, he participated in the Web.com Tour Qualifying School (Q-School), a grueling multistage process that determines which players will earn playing privileges for the upcoming season.

The final stage of the qualifying event saw top amateur and professional golfers from around the world compete for their spot on the Tour. Scottie's performance was solid, placing him among the top 40 finishers, which secured him a number of starts on the Tour.

Qualifying for the Web.com Tour was no small feat. The competition was intense, with many players battling not just for a Tour card, but for the opportunity to launch or rejuvenate their careers. For Scottie, this hard-earned merit was the culmination of years of dedication and a stepping stone toward his ultimate goal of earning a spot on the PGA Tour.

Scottie's success in Q-School wasn't just about earning starts—it was a pivotal moment in his career, marking his transition from a standout college golfer to a professional who could compete at the highest levels. With his tour card in hand, Scottie was ready to make an impact in his first full season as a pro, a promise he'd soon fulfill with a streak of awesome performances that quickly set him apart from his peers.

Scottie's Big Breakthrough

On May 26, 2019, Scottie delivered a performance that catapulted him into the spotlight. Competing in the Evans Scholars Invitational, which was held at The Glen Club in Glenview, Illinois, he fired a bogey-free, 9-under 63 in the final round. This nearly perfect round, where he played the back nine in a blistering 30 strokes, propelled him from six shots behind the leader into a playoff round against Marcelo Rozo.

Scottie's round began with a surge of momentum as he carded three birdies within his first five holes. However, it was on the back nine where he truly caught fire, sinking birdies on holes 10, 11, 13, 14, 15, and 17. His flawless play under pressure was especially notable, as he showed expert levels of poise and skill. He calmly gained a tie for the lead at 17-under 271.

The playoff that followed against Rozo was a test of nerves. Both golfers parred the par-5 18th hole on their first turn; they returned to the same hole for the second playoff. Rozo found himself in trouble, giving Scottie the opening he needed. With precision, Scottie positioned himself perfectly and made a crucial birdie, securing his first Web.com Tour victory.

Reflecting on the win, Scheffler said, "To get the first professional win is awesome, and it kind of gets the monkey off my back" (Chicago Tribune, 2019). This win wasn't just a milestone for Scottie and his family; it was a loud statement that resonated throughout the entire golf world. He had more than proved that he had the composure and ability to close out tournaments, qualities that would continue to serve him well as he marched along his triumphant path to PGA Tour stardom.

This victory, which moved Scheffler up to second on the points list and brought him closer to securing his PGA Tour card for the 2020 season, was the most important moment in his early career. It was a clear indication that the young Texan was ready to take on the challenges of the professional golf world and that bigger things were indeed on the horizon.

Scheffler Wins Again! And the Tour Gets a New Name

Midway through the tour, the tour got a new corporate sponsor. The Web.com tour was now called the Korn Ferry Tour.

On August 18th, Scottie captured his second title on the tour in a stellar performance at the Nationwide Children's Hospital Championship. Taking place at the demanding Scarlet Course of the Ohio State University Golf Club, Scottie carded a final-round 4-under 67 to finish the tournament at 12-under par 272, securing a two-shot victory over his nearest competitors.

This victory marked the beginning of the Korn Ferry Tour Finals, a series of three tournaments that would determine which players would earn their PGA Tour cards for the upcoming season. Scheffler, already assured of his PGA Tour card by finishing third in the regular-season standings, entered the Finals with confidence and ambition, knowing that a strong performance would not only elevate his standing but also provide much-needed momentum heading into the next chapter of his career.

This win propelled Scottie to the top of the playoff standings, positioning him as a strong contender for the coveted fully exempt status on the PGA Tour and a coveted spot in the Players Championship. With this victory, Scottie continued to demonstrate the poise and consistency that he'd had shown in his first breakthrough win on the tour.

As he celebrated his victory with his caddie, Scotty McGuinness, Scottie knew that bigger stages awaited him, but the win in Columbus would remain a huge moment in his journey, again asserting his true potential and signaling his readiness for the next level of competition.

Scottie Named Korn Ferry Tour Player of the Year

At the end of the tour that year, Scottie was named the Korn Ferry Tour Player of the Year, in recognition of his outstanding performances throughout the series. He had already made a big impact on the tour, securing two victories and several other top finishes.

Out of the 21 events during the tour, he made 16 cuts, had six top-five finishes, and placed in the top 10 on 10 different occasions. Not only did Scottie's consistent efforts earn him the Player of the Year title, they also represented a big step toward helping him secure his PGA Tour card for the 2020 season, marking a major milestone in his professional career.

Scottie's success on the Korn Ferry Tour wasn't just about the wins; it was also about the manner in which he played. Scottie's skills were on full display in the final rounds of his two tour victories, where he showed skill and composure, and came out on top.

Reflecting on his Korn Ferry Tour Player of the Year honor, Scottie remained humble and focused on the future, acknowledging the recognition as an important step in his journey but understanding that there was still much to achieve.

As he prepared to transition to the PGA Tour, Scottie carried with him the confidence and momentum built during his successful run on the Korn Ferry Tour. His accomplishments in 2019 not only underscored his potential but also positioned him as a rising star ready to take on the challenges of the PGA Tour, where he would soon make his mark among the best in the world.

The 2020 PGA Tour

Scottie's next stop was the American Express tournament in January 2020. Heading into the final round, he shared the lead with Andrew Landry, both sitting at 21-under par, four strokes ahead of the nearest competitor, Rickie Fowler (Nicholson, 2020). Scottie's performance on the Stadium Course at PGA West, where he shot an impressive 66 in the third round, again proved his ability to handle the pressures of top-level competition.

The Stadium Course, known for its challenging layout and potential hazards, proved to be a true test of Scottie's skills. He navigated the course with precision, avoiding major mistakes and maintaining his position at the top of the leaderboard. Reflecting on the course, Scottie noted, "If you're not on your game, you can really struggle. There's a lot of trouble out there, so you've got to hit a lot of quality shots to keep the ball in play" (The Associated Press, 2020).

A big turning point in Scottie's round came on the par-4 18th hole. After hitting a wayward drive that appeared headed for trouble, he caught a lucky break as the ball bounced off the rocks and into the fairway, allowing him to escape with a par.

Scottie's ability to stay composed under pressure and capitalize on his opportunities showed a growing level of maturity and experience, even though he was just a rookie. Having already secured his PGA Tour card by finishing at the top of the Korn Ferry Tour points list in 2019, he was no stranger to winning. "I think winning is pretty similar at all levels of the game, and I feel like I've done a good job of closing tournaments out, especially last year on the Korn Ferry Tour," Scottie said (The Associated Press, 2020).

Despite the dominance of Dustin Johnson, who won the tournament with 30-under par, Scottie's playing was commendable throughout. His consistency throughout the weekend was evident as he finished tied for fourth place at 17-under par, alongside Kevin Kisner.

Scottie's exceptional performance later that week, where he posted one of the lowest rounds of the day, set the stage for his strong finish. Although he couldn't catch up to Johnson, who was nearly unstoppable, Scottie's fourth-place finish proved that he was one of the most promising rookies of the season.

As Scottie geared up for the final round, he was well on his way toward his first PGA Tour victory, with the confidence and determination that had defined his early career.

Scottie Withdraws From the 120th U.S. Open Due to COVID

In an unexpected turn of events, Scottie had to drop out of the 120th U.S. Open Championship after testing positive for COVID-19. The announcement came just as he was set to compete at Winged Foot Golf Club, a venue known both for its challenging conditions and its historical significance. Even though Scottie was fortunate enough to not have any symptoms from the virus, he had to stay home out of concern for the safety of other golfers.

Scottie's withdrawal was a big loss for the tournament, as he had been enjoying a standout rookie season on the PGA Tour. His performances throughout the year, including a tie for fourth at the PGA Championship and a fifth-place finish at the TOUR Championship, had positioned him as a player to watch at the U.S. Open. This would have been Scheffler's fourth appearance in the U.S. Open, where he had previously made headlines as the low amateur in 2017 at Erin Hills, finishing in a tie for 27th.

The USGA expressed their disappointment at losing a player of Scottie's caliber from the field that year, and fans, friends, and family were saddened to see him quarantined too. Scottie's spot in the competition was taken by Branden Grace, a seasoned pro from South Africa, who was the first alternate based on the Official World Golf Ranking.

For Scottie, the withdrawal must have been a big disappointment for him, especially given the momentum he had built throughout the season. However, his focus remained on health and safety, and he showed lots of maturity in how he handled the situation. As he recuperated at home, Scottie turned his attention to future opportunities, eager to continue his ascent in the world of professional golf.

PGA Rookie of the Year

Despite having had to withdraw from the U.S. Open, Scottie's first season was stellar, and his consistent golfing earned him both the Arnold Palmer Award and the PGA Tour Rookie of the Year. These honors came after a season filled with impressive performances, including seven top-10 finishes, six of which were within the top five, and 13 top-25 placements across 23 events.

Despite not having a single win during the season, Scottie's performances in key tournaments and multiple top-five finishes proved he was among the best golfers on the tour. One of the most memorable highlights of his season was when he shot an incredible 59 during the second round of The Northern Trust, making him one of the few players in PGA Tour history to achieve this feat (Johnson, 2020).

As he reflected on his rookie season, Scottie acknowledged that while he was pleased with his performances, he was hungry for more.

He expressed confidence in his game and his readiness to break through with a win in the next season.

The PGA Tour commissioner, Jay Monahan, praised Scottie for his exceptional season. As Monahan put it: "To follow up Korn Ferry Tour Player of the Year with being voted PGA Tour Rookie of the Year by the PGA Tour membership is an extraordinary achievement and speaks to Scottie's dedication and work ethic" (Johnson, 2020).

Scottie's 2021 Ryder Cup Debut

The Ryder Cup is perhaps the most exciting event in international golf, as the tournament pits the best golfers from the U.S. against their counterparts from Europe in a biennial team competition. The tournament alternates between venues in the U.S. and Europe, and is played following a unique competition format that includes foursomes, four-ball matches, and singles play.

Unlike most golf tournaments, the Ryder Cup isn't so much about the skill of each individual player; it's truly about team effort, national pride, and, often, intense rivalry. The competition is fiercely contested, with players and fans alike deeply invested in the outcome.

The 2021 Ryder Cup, held at Whistling Straits in Wisconsin, was particularly important for Team USA. With a youthful and talented roster, including Scottie, fellow Texan Jordan Spieth, and more, the U.S. team aimed to reclaim the cup after losing in 2018.

The 2021 event featured thrilling matches, passionate displays of sportsmanship, and moments that would forever be etched in Ryder Cup history.

Scottie made an impressive debut in the Cup, contributing to Team USA's dominant performance. Paired with Bryson DeChambeau in the Saturday afternoon four-ball, he played a crucial role in securing a 3-and-

1 victory against Europe's Tommy Fleetwood and Viktor Hovland. This match was a crucial win, as it helped the U.S. team maintain a commanding lead and ultimately set the stage for their overall victory. Scottie's moment of brilliance came during this match when he birdied two consecutive holes, flipping the momentum in favor of the U.S. team after they had been trailing.

The next day of the tournament, Scottie played one of the most challenging singles matches, going head-to-head with world number one, Jon Rahm. He rose to the occasion, defeating Rahm 4-and-3 in a stunning display of skill and composure.

The U.S. team, fueled by performances like Scottie's, went on to win the Ryder Cup with a record margin of 19-9, marking one of the most dominant victories in the event's history. For Scottie, his debut was, simply put, awesome, and it set the tone for what promises to be a successful career in future Ryder Cups.

Don't Forget!

- As a newly minted pro, Scottie hit the ground running, quickly earning his PGA Tour card and the Korn Ferry Tour Player of the Year title.
- Scottie fired an insane 9-under 63 at the Evans Scholars Invitational, clinching his first pro victory.
- Scottie's positive coronavirus test result meant that he had to drop out of the U.S. Open, but he bounced back stronger than ever.
- Named Rookie of the Year for the 2019-2020 PGA Tour season, Scottie proved he was a rising star.
- Scottie made his Ryder Cup debut in 2021, securing a key win against world number one, Jon Rahm. Talk about making an entrance!

Did You Know?

- Scottie likes to have fun, and when he does Karaoke, his go-to track is *Tequila*. Though the song doesn't really have any lyrics besides the word "tequila," we'll still give him a pass due to the fun, party-hardy spirit behind the Mexican melody.
- Scottie says his favorite smell in the world is the smell of bacon being fried up in a pan!

Up Next

Scottie's rookie years showed that he was off to a great start as a gold pro. From earning his Korn Ferry Tour Player of the Year title to being named PGA Tour Rookie of the Year, he proved that he had the talent, drive, and composure to compete with the best in the world. His debut at the Ryder Cup was just the icing on the cake.

As we swing on into the next chapter, we'll follow his rise to the top of the PGA Tour, looking at all the triumphs, challenges, and unforgettable moments that helped him climb to the top.

PART III

Scottie's Ascent to Becoming Number One in the World

CHAPTER 5

❧

Reign of Victory

I think when I'm playing my best, sometimes it feels like I'm competing against myself a little bit out there, trying to keep pushing and stay as focused as I can.

–Scottie Scheffler

The path to becoming a top golfer is one that's filled with many moments of doubt, and constant trials and tribulations. Scottie's rise to golf glory was no exception. But when he found himself on the verge of another big breakthrough in 2022, he kept pushing forward, always keeping his eyes fixed on the prize. Maintaining his positive, forward-looking attitude throughout, he began to dominate the PGA Tour in a way that few could imagine.

In a span of just a few months, he had gone from a rising star to a golfer who could outplay even the most seasoned competitors. The back nine of a tournament, often the make-or-break stretch where champions are defined, became Scottie's proving ground. It was here, amid the pressure and the challenges, that he really started to push himself even harder, securing a series of key victories that would continue to propel his golf career forward.

Scottie's PGA Success

The WM Phoenix Open

The WM Phoenix Open, sometimes called "The People's Open," is a perennial favorite on the PGA Tour. Known for its lively atmosphere and raucous crowds, especially at the infamous 16th hole, the event at TPC Scottsdale in Arizona offers a unique mix of world-class golf and festival-like energy. The 2022 edition of the tournament was no exception, and with all its energy and excitement, it became a fitting stage for Scottie Scheffler's breakthrough PGA victory.

Scottie came into the final round of the tournament trailing the leaders, with little indication that he would be the one hoisting the trophy by the end of the day. The tournament had been dominated by the excellent golfing of other stars, particularly Sahith Theegala, another rookie sensation who took the lead after three rounds. More experienced competitors like Patrick Cantlay and Brooks Koepka were close behind.

Scottie's awesome ability to stay calm under pressure ended up paying off in the final stretch. After an even-par front nine, which included three bogeys, Scottie seemed to be out of the running. But his fortunes changed dramatically as he birdied four of the last six holes, clawing his way back into contention. His putting, which had been commendable, but nothing special throughout the weekend, suddenly shone in the playoff round.

The tournament was ultimately decided in a tense three-hole playoff against Patrick Cantlay, the reigning FedExCup champion. Both Cantlay and Scheffler parred the first two playoff holes, replaying the 18th hole at TPC Scottsdale. On the third trip down the 18th, Scottie sank a dramatic 26-foot birdie putt, a move that put lots of pressure on Cantlay, who missed his 11-foot birdie attempt. With that, Scottie won his first-ever PGA Tour victory in his 71st start, a moment that was as emotional as it was triumphant!

Reflecting on the win, Scottie was quick to acknowledge the significance of his big breakthrough: "I think the first one is probably always the hardest, and I definitely made it pretty difficult on myself today," he said (Schupak, 2022a).

Scottie's big win marked the beginning of what would become an extraordinary season for him, setting the stage for more victories and his eventual rise to the top of the golf world. It was a fitting reward for a player who had long been recognized for his potential but had yet to taste victory on the PGA Tour. Now, with the first win under his belt, golf fans were left wondering just how far Scottie could go.

The Arnold Palmer Invitational

Coming off the high of his first PGA Tour win just weeks earlier, Scottie entered the Arnold Palmer Invitational with momentum and determination. Bay Hill, with its notoriously difficult course conditions and swirling winds, was ready to test every aspect of a golfer's game, and Scottie was up to the challenge.

The tournament was a grind from start to finish. With only four players managing to break par in the final round, it was clear that this would be a battle of mental focus as much as skill.

After starting the final round with two bogeys in the first three holes, Scottie began to face some challenges that would unravel even some of the most experienced golfers. Instead of faltering or languishing though, Scottie steadied himself, showing the composure of a seasoned champion. He played the back nine flawlessly not making a single bogey and adding a crucial birdie on the par-5 12th hole to secure a one-shot lead.

The conditions of the course were brutal, and many of the field's top competitors struggled too. Golf great Rory McIlroy described feeling "punch drunk" after his round, showing just how punishing the course was that day (Schupak, 2022c). Scottie, however, managed to avoid the critical mistakes that cost his competitors dearly. Viktor Hovland and Billy Horschel, who had been in contention, couldn't keep pace with Scottie's steady play, and Gary Woodland, who briefly took the lead, saw his chances slip away with a double bogey on the 17th hole.

Scottie's victory amid these challenging conditions marked his second win in just three starts and propelled him to a career-best of fifth place in the Official World Golf Ranking.

The WGC-Dell Technologies Match Play

Taking place at Austin Country Club, a course familiar to Scheffler from his college days at the University of Texas, at the WGC-Dell Technologies Match Play, Scottie navigated a challenging field with remarkable composure.

In the semifinal round, he faced off against former number-one ranked golfer, Dustin Johnson. Scottie built a commanding 5-up lead through 11 holes, capitalizing on Johnson's struggles on the green.

Johnson mounted a spirited comeback though, winning the next four holes. Despite the pressure, Scottie maintained his lead and secured a 1-up victory after Johnson missed a crucial putt on the 16th hole, ending the match on the 17th.

The final match against Kevin Kisner was a display of Scottie's sheer dominance. He quickly took control, going 3-up through six holes, and never looked back. Kisner, who had not lost a match all week, found himself outplayed and unable to mount a serious challenge. Scottie's confidence and skill were evident as he closed out the match with a 4-and-3 victory.

Scottie's performance throughout the week was characterized by impeccable ball-striking and clutch putting. Notably, he didn't trail in any of his final 57 holes of the tournament, showing his mental fortitude and strategic play.

As Scottie hoisted the trophy above his head, tears started streaming down his face, and he said: "I never got that far in my dreams. I just play golf. I love competing. I'm happy to be out here, you know?" (The Associated Press, 2022b). The win marked another huge milestone in his rapid ascent in the world of golf. With the Masters just around the corner, Scottie's form and confidence made him one of the favorites to don the green jacket at Augusta.

In just over a month, Scottie had gone from a promising talent with no PGA Tour victories to becoming the worldwide top-ranked golfer, with three titles to his name. This awesome achievement came just 42 days after his first PGA Tour win, marking one of the quickest ascents to the top in the history of the OWGR (Scheffler, 2022).

Despite the significance of being named the top golfer in the entire world, Scottie remained grounded, emphasizing that his focus was always on competition rather than rankings. "I don't play for world ranking," he said after his final round at the PGA Championship. "I play to come out here and compete" (*Scheffler Ties for Second, Moves to World No. 1*, 2023).

The Masters

Entering the final round of the 2022 Masters Tournament with a commanding lead, Scottie showed poise and skill as he fended off fierce challenges from Rory McIlroy and other top competitors.

His performance throughout the tournament was extremely strong. By the time Sunday rolled around, he had already established a three-stroke lead. However, his mettle was truly tested during the final round, especially when McIlroy applied pressure with an impressive 8-under 64, tying the record for the lowest final round in Masters history. Despite McIlroy's surge, which included a dramatic chip-in from the bunker on the 18th hole, Scottie maintained his composure.

A defining moment came early in the round on the third hole, where Scottie found himself in trouble after a wayward approach shot. Undeterred, he executed a brilliant chip that rolled perfectly into the hole for birdie. This shot not only extended his lead but also set the tone for the rest of the day, reinforcing his control over the tournament. As the final holes unfolded, Scottie's steady play kept his closest rivals at bay.

By the time Scottie reached the 18th green, his victory was all but assured. Despite a double bogey on the final hole, the result of some uncharacteristic missed putts, his lead was enough to secure a three-stroke victory over McIlroy.

This victory at Augusta was the culmination of a meteoric rise in which Scottie went from a promising young talent to the world's top-ranked golfer. His performance at the Masters underscored his dominance and versatility, as he became the fifth player to win the Masters while holding the world number-one ranking (USA Today Sports, 2022). As he draped the prestigious green jacket over his shoulders, he now found himself among an elite group of legends like Tiger Woods and Dustin Johnson.

Tough Challenges

Missing the Cut: The 2022 PGA Championship

Entering the 2022 PGA Championship as the reigning Masters champion and the world's number-one ranked golfer, expectations were high that

Scottie would continue to dominate. However, the challenging course at Southern Hills Country Club in Tulsa, Oklahoma, had different plans for him.

The tournament began on a sour note for Scottie from the opening round. Despite his usual composed demeanor, he showed rare signs of frustration as he struggled to find his rhythm on the course. He finished the round 1-over par, placing him six shots behind the leader, Rory McIlroy (Morse, 2022). With the pressure mounting, Scottie knew that he needed a strong performance in the second round to make the cut and keep his hopes alive.

On the following day of the tournament, Scottie's grit was on full display as he managed to grind out nine consecutive pars on the front nine. It was clear to everyone though, that he was not playing his best golf. The back nine, however, proved to be his undoing. Consecutive bogeys on the first and second holes of the back nine put him on the defensive, and despite a brief glimmer of hope with a birdie on the 13th, more bogeys followed, sealing his fate.

The final hole of the day summed up Scottie's persistent struggles. After finding a bunker with his tee shot on the par-4 ninth, he compounded the error with a bunker shot that left him just off the green. His ensuing chip was under-hit, leaving him a difficult 15-foot putt for par. When that putt missed, and the subsequent bogey putt also failed to find the hole, Scottie was left to tap in for a double-bogey, capping off a disastrous back nine played in 40 strokes.

Scottie ended the round with a 5-over 75, leaving him six over for the tournament—two strokes above the projected cut line (Morse, 2022). As a result of this, he missed the cut by two strokes—his first missed cut at a major since turning professional. It was also the first time that year that he had recorded consecutive rounds over par, a rare occurrence for a player who had been so consistent throughout the season.

This setback placed Scottie in an unfortunate group of world number-one players who had missed the cut at the Championship. Since the introduction of the world ranking system in 1986, only two others had shared this fate: Seve Ballesteros in 1986 and Dustin Johnson in 2021 (Morse, 2022). For Scottie, the 2022 PGA Championship was a humbling experience, serving as a reminder that even the best in the world can have an off-day on the course.

The Charles Schwab Challenge: Frenemies Forever

Scottie's runner-up finish at the 2022 Charles Schwab Challenge was a reminder of how competitive the world of professional golf can be, even among close friends. In an intense playoff with his friend and rival Sam Burns, Scottie came up just short, losing after Sam holed an amazing 38-foot birdie putt on the first playoff hole (Hawkins, 2022).

Despite Scottie's great golfing, Sam put in an incredible final-round performance. Even though he started the day seven strokes behind Scottie, Sam surged up the leaderboard with a 5-under 65, setting a clubhouse target of 9-under par. As he finished his round and waited, the winds intensified, making life difficult for the other leaders in the tournament, including Scottie.

Scottie had been in control for most of the tournament, carding solid rounds of 66, 65, and 68 in the opening three days. However, in the final round, the gusty conditions at Colonial Country Club took their toll. Scottie struggled to make birdies and ultimately finished with a 2-over 72, managing just enough to force a playoff with three clutch par saves down the stretch.

When the playoffs round began, both players found the fairway on the par-4 18th hole, but it was Sam who seized the moment, leaving

Scottie in the dust. His off-green birdie putt from 38 feet snaked its way into the cup, and unfortunately, Scottie was unable to match it with his 36-foot attempt. Sam's win was his third of the season, moving him to second place in the FedExCup standings, just behind Scottie.

Despite their friendship, both players were fiercely competitive. Scottie acknowledged the unique dynamic between them, saying, "I can assure you, he wanted to beat me more than anybody else and I wanted to beat him more than anybody else" (Schmitt, 2022). For Scottie, the loss was a tough blow, especially after bouncing back from a missed cut at the PGA Championship the previous week. Nonetheless, it highlighted the intensity of their rivalry, which, despite their camaraderie, promises to be a lasting fixture in their careers.

2022 Player of the Year (The Jack Nicklaus Award)

Scottie's four victories during the 2022 tour showed that he was unstoppable. Beyond the statistics, what truly set Scottie apart from other golfers was his consistency. As the season unfolded, he managed to hold onto the top spot in the FedExCup standings for 24 weeks, dominating both the early and middle portions of the year (*Scottie Scheffler Wins Jack Nicklaus Award as PGA Tour Player of the Year*, 2022).

Although he narrowly missed out on a few more wins, including a runner-up finish at the Tour Championship, Scottie's sustained excellence resonated with his peers, leading to him securing the Player of the Year honor with 89 percent of the vote (Melton, 2022).

By the time the season concluded, Scottie had recorded 11 top-10 finishes and amassed over $14 million in official earnings, the highest in PGA Tour history at the time (*Scottie Scheffler Wins Jack Nicklaus Award as PGA Tour Player of the Year*, 2022).

The Jack Nicklaus Award, which is presented every year to the PGA Tour Player of the Year, represents one of the highest honors in professional golf, and winning it for the first time in 2022 was a career-defining moment for Scheffler. The award was particularly special because it reflected the respect and recognition of his fellow players on tour.

Scottie's Jack Nicklaus Award was presented in a unique and memorable way. During an appearance on ESPN's *College GameDay* at his alma mater, the University of Texas, Scottie was surprised with the trophy on stage. The emotional moment came in front of a cheering crowd, with his former college coach by his side.

The 2022 Presidents Cup

Scottie's awesome golfing earned him a coveted spot on the U.S. team for the 2022 Presidents Cup. His automatic qualification came as no surprise after his four PGA Tour victories, including his first major win at the Masters.

Scottie finished the qualification process as the top-ranked golfer in the U.S. team standings, collecting 13,180 points, a big margin ahead of his peers (Schupak, 2022d).

Heading into the event, the expectations for Scottie were high. As the top-ranked player in the world, he was seen as a crucial part of the U.S. team's strategy to hold onto the Presidents Cup at Quail Hollow Club in Charlotte. His performance in international competitions, such as the previous year's Ryder Cup, had already shown his ability to rise to the occasion in team formats, as he had become a valuable asset for U.S. team captain Davis Love III.

In interviews, Love praised Scheffler's competitiveness and noted that his experiences from the Ryder Cup would make him even more of a powerful force on the Presidents Cup team.

Despite his stellar year, Scottie's playing at the Presidents Cup proved to be more challenging than anticipated. Partnering with his frenemy Sam Burns, the pair faced some tough opponents and unexpected struggles. Though both of them had been dominant in many PGA Tour events, during the Presidents Cup, they found themselves on the losing end of several matches.

Scottie's struggles reached a low point during one particularly tough shot, where he hit a shank off the tee. The errant shot reminded the spectators and other golfers that golf can humble anyone at any time.

However, setbacks like these did little to diminish the overall significance of Scottie's presence on the U.S. team. Despite some difficulties, his competitive spirit and contributions in key moments were crucial, as the U.S. team went on to dominate the competition. In the end, the U.S. team secured the Presidents Cup that year.

Starting 2023 With a Bang

The 2023 WM Phoenix Open

Scottie's 2023 season got off to a strong start as he was able to defend his title at the WM Phoenix Open in February. At TPC Scottsdale, he showed composure on the course, overcoming challenges to claim his fifth PGA Tour victory and regain the number-one ranking. In a thrilling final round, he posted a bogey-free 6-under 65 to finish at 19-under 265, two strokes ahead of Canadian golfer Nick Taylor (The Associated Press, 2023c).

Scottie's performance at the tournament was marked by key moments, most notably a 22-foot eagle putt on the par-5 13th hole, which broke a tie with Taylor and put him firmly in the lead (The Associated Press, 2023a). On the iconic 16th hole, after a wayward tee shot, Scottie managed to drain a 15-foot par putt to maintain his advantage. This steady play solidified his lead, and he closed with a birdie on the 17th, clinching his victory.

"I knew it was going to take a great round," Scottie said after the win (Schupak, 2023a). "Nobody was going to give this golf tournament to me. I had to go out and earn it" (Schupak, 2023a). This victory allowed him to reclaim the top spot in the Official World Golf Ranking, surpassing Rory McIlroy, and solidifying his standing as one of the most dominant players on tour (Yadav, 2023).

Scottie's back-to-back victories at the WM Phoenix Open put him in rare company, making him just the seventh player to defend his title in the tournament's history (Scheffler, 2023a). This feat placed him alongside legends such as Ben Hogan, Arnold Palmer, and Hideki Matsuyama.

The Players Championship

Scottie's awesome run in 2023 continued with his commanding victory at the Players Championship in March. With a stellar showing, he managed to secure his sixth career win and his first Players Championship title. His consistency and skill were on full display at TPC Sawgrass, where he shot a 3-under 69 on the final day to finish 17-under 271, claiming victory by an impressive five-shot margin. This marked the largest margin of victory in the tournament since Stephen Ames' six-shot win in 2006 (The Associated Press, 2023b).

Scottie's dominance was apparent throughout the tournament, especially during the final round, when he delivered a stunning run of five consecutive birdies starting at the 8th hole. His aggressive approach on the par-4 12th hole, where he opted to drive the green rather than lay up showed his high level of confidence and self-belief. This bold strategy paid off as he built an insurmountable lead and cruised to victory, leaving his competitors trailing in his wake.

The win also made Scheffler only the third player, alongside golf legends Jack Nicklaus and Tiger Woods, to hold both the Masters Tournament and the Players Championship titles simultaneously (Scheffler, 2023). His triumph at Sawgrass meant that he was again ranked number one in the world.

Grandma Knows Best

Scottie's victory at the Players Championship was a family affair, as he celebrated on the 18th green with his wife, Meredith, his parents, Diane and Scott, and his 87-year-old grandmother, who had followed him throughout the day. For Scottie, the victory was hard-won, and the glory was mighty tasty, almost as satisfying as his grandma's famous chocolate pie.

Scottie's relationship with his grandma, Mary Delorenzo, in fact, is a heartwarming aspect of his personal life, which remains an anchor amid his growing fame and success in the golf world. At 88 years old, Mary has become something of a legend herself, famously following her grandson for all 72 holes during his triumphant win at the 2023 Players Championship. Her dedication to supporting Scottie caught the attention of fans and the media, but neither Scottie nor his grandma were aware of the viral fame she gained as she strolled alongside the course. Despite the attention, Scottie and Grandma Mary remain unfazed by the hype, sharing a bond rooted in simplicity and family values.

Let's take a minute to talk about Grandma Mary's famous chocolate cream pie, a dessert that Scottie is reported to adore like no other dessert. After his victories, Scottie often celebrates with a meal at his grandma's house, just a short drive from TPC Sawgrass outside of Jacksonville, Florida.

Grandma Mary's pie is a family favorite, and although the clubhouse at Sawgrass attempted their own version of it, Scottie is adamant about the fact that nothing compares to his grandmother's original recipe, which he jokingly credits for making him gain a few extra pounds after every visit.

The 2023 Ryder Cup

But all the sweetness of Grandma Mary's pie could not make up for the bitterness ahead. The 2023 Ryder Cup in Rome turned out to be one of the toughest moments of Scottie Scheffler's career, both emotionally and professionally. He entered the competition as one of the world's top-ranked golfers, but the event would soon leave him visibly shaken.

Paired with five-time major champion Brooks Koepka, Scottie faced a humbling defeat in the foursomes match. Koepka and Scheffler were soundly beaten 9&7 by Europe's Viktor Hovland and rookie Ludvig Åberg, marking the largest margin of victory ever recorded in an 18-hole Ryder Cup match (Bantock, 2023; Stafford, 2023).

The match was over by the 11th hole, leaving both American golfers reeling from their performance. They had struggled from the outset, falling three down after just three holes due to a series of double bogeys and missed opportunities. In contrast, Hovland and Åberg played near-flawless golf, rolling in birdies on six consecutive holes. The Europeans were simply unstoppable, while Scottie and Brooks just could not seem to find their rhythm (Stafford, 2023).

For Scottie, the crushing loss hit hard. Sitting on the back of a golf cart after the match, he was seen in tears, his emotions spilling over as Meredith came over to console him. It was a raw display of vulnerability from the typically composed player, showing just how much the Ryder Cup meant to him (Bantock, 2023).

Adding to the sting was the fact that this defeat came on the heels of another difficult match. On Friday afternoon, Scottie and Koepka had been poised to claim a point for the U.S. team, only for Jon Rahm to steal a tie with two late eagles (Bantock, 2023). Scottie's frustration grew as the weekend progressed, with his personal struggles on the course reflecting the broader difficulties faced by Team USA.

In the end, Scottie's disappointment at the Ryder Cup was really uncharacteristic of him. The botched team effort was a stark contrast to his individual successes earlier in the season. Despite his incredible run of form in 2023, including victories at the WM Phoenix Open and the Players Championship, the Ryder Cup proved to be a different beast. The emotional toll of the defeat, coupled with the immense pressure of representing his country, showed just how much pressure was on Scottie and his teammates. It was something even a delicious chocolate pie from grandma's house could not fix.

Getting Back Up: Winning the Hero World Challenge

After a challenging season that included both personal highs and competitive lows, Scottie closed out 2023 on a triumphant note by taking the prize in the Hero World Challenge. The event, hosted by Tiger Woods, invites top golfers from all around the world to come together for some friendly competition.

Although the title doesn't count toward official PGA Tour statistics, the tournament offers world ranking points and an opportunity for players to test their skills against some of the best in the game.

For Scottie, winning Tiger's invitational was more than just another trophy—it marked a return to form and a re-assertion of his core strengths. Having finished as the runner-up in the Hero World Challenge for the two previous years, Scottie approached the event with determination.

Held at Albany Golf Course in Nassau, Bahamas, Tiger's tournament was a final chance to reflect on the progress he had made throughout the year, particularly in overcoming the struggles with his putting, which had plagued him in previous tour appearances.

Scottie's performance throughout the Hero World Challenge was awesome. He played a bogey-free final round, finishing with a 4-under par 68 and a total score of 20-under 268. This score gave him a comfortable three-shot victory over Sepp Straka, who made a late push with a final-round 64 but could not overcome Scottie's commanding lead. Justin Thomas finished another stroke behind in third place.

Much of Scottie's success in the Hero World Challenge can be attributed to his improved putting, a weakness that had been a consistent issue for him throughout the entire season. Earlier in the year, despite leading in several key statistical categories such as strokes gained from tee to green, his struggles on the green had kept him from converting more opportunities into wins.

Determined to address his perceived deficit on the green, Scottie began working with renowned putting coach Phil Kenyon. The results were immediate, as his putting performance at the Hero World Challenge was a key factor in his win.

Even when rivals like Straka and Thomas tried to close the gap, Scottie was able to stay focused and executed birdies at critical moments. He missed only one putt from inside five feet throughout the entire tournament, showing that clear progress had been made. Reflecting on his performance, Scheffler said: "I was just trying to hit good shots and get as many looks as I could for birdies" (*Scottie Scheffler Wins Hero World Challenge; Tiger Woods Finishes 18th*, 2023).

This win capped off a year in which Scottie had faced various ups and downs, including the heartbreaking loss at the Ryder Cup just a few months earlier. Yet, through it all, he remained committed to improving his game. His Hero World Challenge victory announced to the world that he was ready for the challenges that lay ahead in the next season.

In the end, the Hero World Challenge win was a fitting conclusion to Scottie's year. It was a tough year, but it was one marked by lessons learned, adjustments made, and a determination to get back up stronger than ever.

Continuing His Winning Ways in 2024

The Arnold Palmer Invitational

Scottie's return to Bay Hill for the 2024 Arnold Palmer Invitational was a triumphant one, as he got his second victory at the event. After all the effort Scottie had put into refining his putting skills, this year he's taken a simpler approach to his game, focusing on executing his stroke without the pressure of seeking perfection. That mindset shift paid off in a big way at Bay Hill.

Scottie dominated at the Arnold Palmer, especially in his final round, when he fired a bogey-free 6-under 66 to win by five strokes. This victory reminded some commentators of Tiger Woods' win in 2012, which was also achieved with a five-shot margin.

All Scottie's putting practice paid off, and he didn't miss a single putt within 15 feet over the course of the competition (Ferguson, 2024b).

Leading in numerous stats already, Scottie was tied for the lead with Shane Lowry. While his rivals, including U.S. Open champion Wyndham Clark, struggled with the course's challenging conditions, Scottie thrived.

He made key birdies at crucial moments and used his newfound confidence on the greens to pull away from the field. By the back nine, the tournament was all but over, with Scheffler holding a commanding five-shot lead that he never relinquished.

Scottie's decision to switch to a more forgiving mallet putter, combined with a shift in mindset, allowed him to overcome the struggles that had plagued his game. As he noted after the victory, "I did a really good job of not letting the misses get to me" (Ferguson, 2024b).

The win at the Arnold Palmer was Scottie's seventh on the PGA Tour, and it further served to reinforce his position as the world's top-ranked golfer. It was a timely reminder of his ability to dominate, especially on difficult courses like Bay Hill. With this win, Scottie effectively silenced any doubts about his putting abilities, including the self-doubts that caused him to actively work on his putting skills in the first place.

The Masters

Scottie's Masters victory marked an important milestone in his career, as he captured his second green jacket in just three years. Winning by four shots over Ludvig Åberg, he delivered a performance that underscored his status as one of the game's best. Entering the final round with a narrow one-shot lead, Scottie managed to separate himself from the competition by shooting a 4-under par 68, finishing the tournament at 11-under.

At just 27 years old, Scottie became the fourth-youngest player in history to win two Masters titles, placing him among the elite company of Jack Nicklaus, Tiger Woods, and Seve Ballesteros. His ability to maintain composure and execute crucial shots throughout the back nine, particularly with birdies on the par-5 13th and par-4 14th holes, allowed him to pull away from the field and secure the victory.

Ludvig Åberg, in his Masters debut, posed a real threat throughout the tournament, but a critical mistake on the 11th hole, where he found the water and made a double bogey, opened the door for Scottie to extend his lead. Despite Åberg's impressive performance, Scottie remained unflappable, showing his signature consistency and control.

The RBC Heritage

Scottie's 2024 success streak did not end at Augusta. Just one week later, he continued his streak by winning the RBC Heritage at Hilton Head Island. It was his fourth victory in just five starts.

Held at Harbour Town Golf Links, the tournament again put Scottie's consistency on display, as he finished the tournament with a score of 19-under par, three strokes ahead of runner-up Sahith Theegala. His victory came after a weather delay forced the final round to extend into Monday, but Scottie remained unfazed, completing the last three holes with precision.

This victory made him the first player to win both the Masters and the RBC Heritage in consecutive weeks since Bernhard Langer in 1985 (Douglas, 2024). It was a rare accomplishment, with only one other player, Tiger Woods in 2006, winning a tournament immediately following a major victory. Scottie's win in Hilton Head reasserted his dominance while solidifying his place as the world's top-ranked golfer, with all 10 of his PGA Tour victories occurring within the past 26 months.

The highlight of Scottie's performance at the RBC Heritage was his spectacular third-round score of 63, which set up his victory. The consistency that had characterized his season, from his ball striking to his improved putting, was again evident, as he held off strong challenges from the likes of Wyndham Clark, Patrick Cantlay, and Justin Thomas.

Scottie's parents, Scott and Diane, were there to witness their son's historic achievement, proudly celebrating his victory. Their sacrifices had played a pivotal role in his development as a golfer, as they had gone to extreme lengths, even taking out loans, to ensure Scottie could access top-tier training when he was a kid.

Reflecting on his victory at the RBC Heritage, Scottie said: "I didn't show up here just to have some sort of ceremony and have people tell me congratulations. I came here with a purpose" (Douglas, 2024).

An Eventful 2024 PGA Championship

At the 2024 PGA Championship, Scottie showed strength despite a series of off-course events that could have easily derailed his performance. Scottie's last round 65 at Valhalla Golf Club marked a return to form after a challenging and tumultuous week.

He entered the event having not competed for three weeks, as he was spending time with Meredith, after the birth of their first son. Despite this family milestone in the weeks leading up to the Championship, Scottie encountered an unexpected obstacle in the form of a run-in with the law.

The Unfortunate Incident

Scottie's arrest was a result of a chaotic misunderstanding. As he was trying to enter Valhalla Golf Club early in the morning, the roads were blocked due to a fatal accident involving a shuttle bus. In the confusion, he drove past a police roadblock, leading to an altercation with a police officer.

The officer claimed that Scottie refused to comply with traffic instructions, causing him to be detained on charges of second-degree assault on a police officer, reckless driving, and ignoring traffic signals (Beall, 2024). The arrest report claimed that Scottie drove forward despite being instructed not to, which allegedly resulted in the officer being dragged to the ground.

After the dust had settled, the officer was taken to the hospital with minor injuries, including pain and abrasions. However, Scottie maintained that he was simply following the directions of another officer who said he could drive forward, leading to confusion during the chaotic scene.

Even though Scottie didn't physically attack the officer, and meant no harm, the charges were based on the alleged failure to comply and the movement of the vehicle, not on any real physical altercation that occurred between them.

Scottie later described the situation as a "big misunderstanding," (Haworth, 2024). The entire incident left him shaken, and he admitted to feeling confused and scared while in custody. Scottie's attorney, Steve Romines, supported his claim of innocence, noting that the golfer was just following traffic directions and wasn't intentionally disregarding any orders.

Despite the arrest, Scottie managed to stay composed, crediting his ability to focus on his game. After being released, he arrived at Valhalla just before his tee time.

The arrest understandably impacted Scottie's mental state. However, after being released without bail, he managed to regroup, shooting an impressive 66 in his second round. His ability to remain composed during this difficult situation earned him widespread praise, especially during his post-round interview, where he redirected attention to the tragic accident that had initially caused the police presence and praised the officers involved.

This ability to compartmentalize these issues revealed a deep mental strength. Despite the physical and emotional toll of the arrest, he managed to stay competitive, finishing the first round near the top of the leaderboard.

By the third round, however, Scottie began to struggle. With his regular caddie, Ted Scott, absent due to his daughter's high school graduation, Scottie instead was accompanied by substitute caddie Brad Payne. This arrangement had been discussed well in advance, as both Scottie and Ted had agreed that family takes precedence over work.

Scottie trusted Brad, especially for tasks like raking bunkers, and believed his experience on tour would ensure a smooth experience despite the temporary switch. The disruption to his routine though, combined with the exhaustion of the prior events, led to an uncharacteristic 73, ending his streak of 42 consecutive rounds under par in major championships (Martin, 2024). He managed to bounce back with a 6-under 65 in the final round.

Despite the difficulties he found on the course, Scottie's fighting spirit prevailed in the final round. After a bogey on the first hole, he went on to record seven birdies and no further mistakes, finishing the championship at 13-under par and securing a top-10 finish. His determination and mental toughness were clear as he reflected on the week. Even though he admitted to being tired, he fought through the challenges.

Scottie Sr. and Diane's reaction to their son's shocking arrest was a mix of disbelief and concern, as they learned about the situation in real-time through media coverage.

During his brief imprisonment, Scottie was let out of the jail cell momentarily for his phone call. He called his parents and reassured them that he was okay and that the whole thing was a big misunderstanding. During the conversation, Scottie Sr. offered some comforting advice, encouraging his son to maintain respect and be himself, despite the chaos of the situation.

Randy Smith praised the composure of Scottie's parents, noting that many would have panicked in a similar situation. The family's approach to the ordeal reflected the calm and grounded nature that Scottie is known for on and off the course.

In the aftermath, Diane expressed a broader perspective. From all her years in corporate law, she was well aware of the fact that misunderstandings like this can happen anywhere, and that communication is key to resolving such issues.

Continuing Onward

In the wake of the incident at the PGA Championship, Scottie trudged onward.

The Charles Schwab Challenge

In the 2024 edition of the Charles Schwab Challenge, Scottie aimed for another strong showing, especially after all his recent successes.

Playing close to his Dallas home, he entered the final round trailing Davis Riley, who had established a four-stroke lead. Scottie struggled to gain momentum, particularly in the windy conditions, and didn't manage a birdie until the 13th hole (The Associated Press, 2024b).

Despite his best efforts, he couldn't seem to apply enough pressure on Riley, who remained composed throughout the round. Riley's bogey on the second hole was the only hiccup before he quickly responded with a birdie on the fourth, widening his lead. By the ninth hole, he had extended his lead over Scottie to six strokes.

Ultimately, Scottie finished with a 71, five strokes behind Riley, marking his third consecutive top-three finish at the Charles Schwab Challenge. Although he couldn't clinch the title, Scottie's consistency continued to shine, with this result being his 11th top-10 finish in 12 tournaments that year.

The Memorial Tournament

Scottie secured his fifth win of the 2024 season with a dramatic victory at the Memorial Tournament. Played at the prestigious Muirfield Village Golf Club, he faced tough competition and challenging conditions, but his steady performance throughout the tournament set him apart. He started the final round with a four-shot lead but found himself battling to hold onto his advantage as Collin Morikawa closed the gap.

On the 18th hole, both golfers found the rough after their approach shots bounced off the green. Scottie remained composed, sinking a critical five-foot par putt to clinch a one-stroke victory at 8-under par.

This win added another $4 million to his season earnings, pushing his total prize money for the year to over $24 million, setting a new PGA Tour record (Badenhausen, 2024).

The Travelers Championship

At the 2024 Travelers Championship, Scottie secured his sixth win of the season by defeating Tom Kim in a sudden-death playoff. Both golfers finished regulation tied at 22-under par, with Kim sinking a birdie putt on the 72nd hole, forcing a playoff round.

Despite Kim's excellent golfing, Scottie remained composed, hitting a stellar approach on the first playoff hole, while Kim faltered with a difficult bunker shot. Scottie's two-putt par sealed the victory, continuing his dominant season.

This marked Scottie's 12th career PGA Tour title and solidified his status as the top-ranked golfer in the world. The win earned him $3.6 million, bringing his 2024 earnings to over $27 million (Peters, 2024).

In addition to gaining individual recognition, Scottie's victory at the Travelers further boosted his standing atop the U.S. Presidents Cup team rankings.

The 2024 Olympics

In his Olympic debut at the 2024 Paris Games, Scottie added to his remarkable year by winning the gold medal in men's golf. Starting the final round four strokes behind leaders Jon Rahm and Xander Schauffele, he mounted a captivating comeback. Shooting a 62 at Le Golf National, he completed a 9-under par round, driven by an incredible birdie streak on the back nine, including four consecutive birdies. This incredible performance made Scottie tied for the all-time course record.

While Rahm had established a commanding lead early on, he faltered on the back nine with back-to-back bogeys and a costly double bogey at the 14th hole. Meanwhile, Scottie capitalized on this opening, surging up the leaderboard with a string of birdies. His par save on the 13th hole and a critical approach shot on the 15th helped him maintain momentum, ultimately sealing the victory with a total score of 19-under par.

The winning of an Olympic gold medal represented another big moment for him. Reflecting on the achievement, Scottie expressed deep pride in representing the United States and described the experience of standing on the podium with a gold medal as something he would "remember for a long time" (Stats Perform, 2024).

Don't Forget!

- Scottie's competitive battle with friend Sam Burns at the Charles Schwab Challenge reminded everyone that even friendships get tested on the course.

- Scottie added six titles to his collection, including major wins at the Masters and the Players Championship.
- Scottie golfed with a substitute caddie during a critical round at the PGA Championship and still managed a top-10 finish.
- Despite a bizarre run-in with law enforcement during the PGA Championship, Scottie stayed focused and delivered top-tier performances.

Did You Know?

- Scottie wears a US men's size 11.5 shoe (45 European).
- Like E.T., the Extraterrestrial, he loves Reese's Pieces candy.
- He eats Chipotle a lot, probably more than any other fast food chain.
- Even though he has tons of money, he still drives an older model car that his dad gave him.

Up Next

From earning his second Masters title to overcoming personal challenges off the course, Scottie showed that greatness isn't just about talent but also about mental toughness and composure under pressure. His gold-medal win at the Paris Olympics was the crowning jewel in a year filled with some truly awesome achievements.

As we wrap up this chapter, it's clear that Scottie's momentum is far from slowing down. But with the heights he's reached, what comes next? In the following chapter, we'll recap Scottie's career thus far and try to find the formulas behind his stunning level of success in global golf.

CHAPTER 6

※

Celebrating the Past and Embracing the Future

You just do the best that you can and with the hand you're dealt and just go from there.

–Scottie Scheffler

From his first PGA Tour victory in 2022 to becoming one of the sport's dominant figures by 2024, Scottie has steadily carved out a place among the all-time golf greats. His achievements include multiple major titles, prestigious championships, and record-setting earnings, all of which have firmly cemented his place in golf history.

With 12 PGA Tour victories to his name, Scottie has proven time and again that he is a force to be reckoned with. His big breakthrough at the 2022 WM Phoenix Open, his Arnold Palmer Invitational win, and his victory at the WGC-Dell Technologies Match Play all propelled him forward. These victories paved the way for what would be his crowning achievement of the season: his first Masters victory in 2022. Then came his triumph at Augusta National and his back-to-back wins at the 2023 WM Phoenix Open and the Players Championship.

As we saw in the previous chapter, the 2024 season has been equally impressive for Scottie. With victories at the Arnold Palmer Invitational, his second Masters title, and the RBC Heritage, he's shown that his form is as consistent as ever. His ability to perform on golf's biggest stages has not only earned him multiple championships but has also placed him in the upper echelon of all-time PGA Tour earnings. By mid-2024, Scottie had surpassed $70 million in career earnings, placing him fifth on the all-time money list (Kelly, 2024).

Scottie's contributions to U.S. national appearances, such as the Presidents Cup and Ryder Cup, have been invaluable. His teamwork and competitive spirit in doubles and team competitions have made him a key asset in U.S. golf. With years of golf ahead of him, there's no telling how many more records he'll break or how many more victories he'll claim. *But how has Scottie made it this far?* In this chapter, we'll find out.

What's the Secret Behind Scottie Scheffler's Success?

Scottie Scheffler's rise to the top of the golf world was no accident. His success stems from a combination of support from his family, physical preparation, mental strength, and his Christian faith, each of which plays a vital role in his sustained dominance on the PGA Tour.

Off-Course Preparation: Fitness as a Foundation

One of the major factors behind Scottie's success is his dedication to physical conditioning, something that became a priority after a bout with back pain during his college years. Under the guidance of his long-time performance coach, Dr. Troy Van Biezen, Scheffler adopted a comprehensive fitness regimen focused on preventing injury and building endurance. This shift allowed him to avoid the aches and pains that previously hampered his performance.

Scottie's training program is centered on metabolic, hypertrophy, and strength exercises, incorporating tools such as skiers, rowers, and Wattbikes for cardiovascular conditioning. His increased endurance, built through consistent work off the course, has given him the stamina needed to maintain his edge in those pressure-packed moments on the course. A key component of his routine includes *GolfForever*, a training system that focuses on mobility and stability while minimizing the risk of injury.

Tackling the Mental Game

While physical preparation has been essential for Scottie, his mental game is arguably his greatest asset. His approach to golf is rooted in patience and the ability to remain calm under pressure. Whether dealing with a tough lie or recovering from a mistake, Scottie stays composed, reminding himself of all that he's done to prepare, and trusting the work he's done.

This mental toughness has been especially important in managing his emotions during high-stakes tournaments like the Masters. Scottie has mastered the art of letting go, moving on from errors, and maintaining focus on the next shot. By channeling his nerves into positive energy, he enhances his focus when the pressure is highest, a trait that has helped him pull off dramatic victories.

The Technical Edge: Shot Shaping and Putting

On a technical level, Scottie's ability to shape shots is another key to his dominance. His versatility on the course allows him to hit a variety of shot shapes, including his signature draw, which he executes by slightly closing his stance and focusing on turning over his trail forearm. This attention to detail and precision in practice ensures that he's never experimenting during competition. Every shot he hits in a tournament is one he's rehearsed countless times.

Scottie's improved putting has also been crucial to his success, as he's continually made adjustments to his technique over time, and has focused on being more visual with his approach. Instead of relying on the alignment lines on his ball, he now visualizes the path of the putt, which has helped him eliminate confusion and improve his consistency.

Faith as a Driving Force

One of the biggest influences on Scottie's career has been his faith. His devout Catholic beliefs have provided him with a sense of peace and security, helping him keep his priorities in order. He often emphasizes that while he loves winning, his identity is not tied to his performance on the golf course. This mindset frees him from the burden of outcome-driven pressure, allowing him to play with a sense of calm that many competitors struggle to achieve.

Scottie often attributes his ability to stay grounded and focused, even during the most intense moments, to the belief that his ultimate success is predestined. As he once put it: "My buddies told me this morning my victory was secure on the cross" (*Scottie Scheffler's Not so Secret Weapon*, 2024).

Looking Toward the Future

The 2025 PGA Tour season is shaping up to be one of continuity and excitement for Scottie, with many signature events and established tournaments returning to the schedule. The upcoming season promises to feature a balance of high-stakes competitions and familiar venues.

After what's so far been a busy 2024 season, which included a reevaluation of his preparation strategies following the U.S. Open, Scottie's focus for 2025 seems to be on fine-tuning his schedule, particularly around major championships.

Scottie's approach to both the Byron Nelson and Charles Schwab Challenge will be influenced by his desire to optimize his performance throughout the season, while also continuing to make time for family and personal commitments, which have taken on increasing importance for Scotty, especially since the birth of his son, Bennett.

Although his professional ambitions remain strong, in recent interviews, Scottie has been candid about how, as a new dad, his priorities are shifting. He has made it clear that his family will always come first, and he is prepared to make adjustments in his golfing schedule to spend more time at home.

From a purely logistical and game-prep standpoint, Scottie's plans for 2025 are set to see a reevaluation of his overall tournament preparation strategy, following a challenging 2024 U.S. Open. After struggling to adapt to the course conditions at Pinehurst No. 2, Scottie admitted that playing the week before such a demanding event may not have been ideal.

He has also been up front about the fact that competing in events like the Memorial Tournament, hosted by Jack Nicklaus, required substantial effort on a course, often approaching the preparation required for a major championship setup. This led him to conclude that his preparation might have been more effective had he spent that time resting and fine-tuning his game at home.

In light of this experience, Scottie has already said that he'll consider skipping events before major tournaments in 2025, especially in the lead-up to the U.S. Open. His performance in 2024 demonstrated that intense back-to-back competitions can be taxing, and he plans to manage his schedule more carefully to ensure peak performance when it matters most.

Scottie's strategy for 2025 and beyond appears to be one that will focus on finding a balance between maintaining his competitive edge and ensuring adequate recovery time, with particular emphasis on arriving at major tournaments feeling well prepared both mentally and physically.

Future Hall of Fame Potential?

Scottie's name has been frequently thrown around in discussions about the future of the World Golf Hall of Fame. His rapid rise to world number one, coupled with multiple major victories, has placed him on a trajectory to join the prestigious ranks of golfing legends. With two Masters titles, Players Championship victories, and consistent top-10 finishes, Scottie's career achievements make him a strong contender for future induction.

The World Golf Hall of Fame itself is undergoing significant changes, with discussions about relocating and modernizing its presentation of the sport's history. As the Hall of Fame looks to the future, young potential inductees like Scottie represent a new era of golf mastery.

Don't Forget!

- Scottie Scheffler won two Masters titles in just three seasons.
- By 2024, Scottie's career earnings topped $70 million, placing him 5th on the all-time money list (Kelly, 2024).

- Scottie focuses on metabolic, hypertrophy, and strength exercises to stay in shape.
- Scottie's secret to success lies in his ability to move on from mistakes quickly and stay focused on the next shot, while his Christian faith gives him peace and perspective.

Did You Know?

- Scottie has had one hole-in-one (*Scottie Scheffler Career Hole in Ones*, 2024).

Up Next

So, you might be wondering what lies beyond the horizon for Scottie off the course? In the next chapter, we'll take a look at Scottie's personal life. From his deep-rooted family values and spiritual beliefs to his charitable work, we'll take a look at how these elements have shaped and will continue to inform his life and career.

PART IV

Scottie's Personal Life and Other Endeavors

CHAPTER 7

※

Beyond the Golf Course

*My identity isn't a golf score. Like Meredith told me this morning,
if you win this golf tournament today, if you lose this golf tournament by
10 shots...I'm still going to love you, you're still going to be the
same person, Jesus loves you and nothing changes.*

–Scottie Scheffler

Marriage and Family Life

Scottie and Meredith's love story began long before his golf career reached global fame. The two had been high school sweethearts at Highland Park High School, and tied the knot in December 2020. Together, they navigated things long distance while pursuing their respective college educations—Scottie at the University of Texas and Meredith at Texas A&M.

Throughout their college years, they managed to maintain a strong connection, always looking toward a future together. Their bond, deeply rooted in shared Christian values and faith, became a source of strength for Scottie as his career soared.

Meredith has stood by Scottie's side through his many career milestones, from attending tournaments to caddying for him in the Par 3 Contest at the Masters in 2022. As Scottie captured his first major title at that very Masters tournament, he credited her for keeping him grounded. In moments of doubt or pressure, it was Meredith's calm reassurance that helped him remain focused.

Following their marriage, Scottie and Meredith purchased a $2.1 million home in Dallas, Texas, where they now reside. This 5,000-square-foot house, nestled in the upscale Devonshire neighborhood, boasts five bedrooms and six bathrooms. Despite his growing wealth—bolstered by multiple PGA Tour victories and sponsorships—the house, though very large, still fits with the Schefflers' modest and grounded lifestyle, as they likely plan to have more children.

The home is filled with amenities that offer a perfect retreat from the demands of professional golf. Its spacious master bedroom comes with his-and-hers closets and a cozy sitting area. Outside, the half-acre lot features a backyard, complete with a covered patio, fireplace, and pool (Fenner, 2024). Purchased in 2020, the home has since appreciated in value, now estimated to be worth over $3 million (Jacob, 2024).

This home has become more than just a living space—it's where the couple has built their life together, balancing the demands of Scottie's career with the joys of family life. The house also serves as a great play place for baby Bennett as he grows up. Maybe Scottie and Bennett will even play golf in the backyard at night by flashlight, just as he did with his dad as a kid.

Baby Bennett

Baby Bennett's birth came just weeks after Scottie claimed his second Masters title in April. The couple shared the news of their baby's arrival with a heartwarming Instagram post, where Scottie cradled his newborn son in his arms, expressing, "Your mom and dad love you so much" (McKnight, 2024).

Leading up to Bennett's birth, Scottie managed to balance the pressures of his professional career with the anticipation of becoming a father. Despite competing at the highest level during the 2024 Masters, he had made it clear that if Meredith went into labor, he was fully prepared to withdraw from the tournament.

As he put it, "I think the first child wins...over many things in my life" (Andres, 2024). Fortunately, the timing worked out perfectly, and he was able to secure his second green jacket before heading home to be with Meredith and their new child.

Scottie has remained focused on both family and professional responsibilities. He shared his awe at watching Meredith's progress throughout her pregnancy and the birthing process, describing it as a "wild ride" and expressing immense pride in her strength (Staff, 2024).

Faith and Devotion

Scottie's Catholic faith has remained a core part of his life, providing a solid foundation that guides both his personal and professional decisions. Raised in a decidedly Christian household, he's never shied away from expressing the central role that faith plays in his journey.

Scottie has made it clear in interviews that his purpose is much larger than just his success in golf. As he put it: "All I'm trying to do is glorify God and that's why I'm here and that's why I'm in position" (SK Desk, 2024c).

In various interviews, Scottie has made it clear that his faith in Jesus is what ultimately defines him as a person, not all the successes he's had on the course. This mindset helps him maintain balance amid the highs and lows of professional golf. As he explained before the 2024 Masters, golf is important, but it does not define who he is. His identity is firmly grounded in his relationship with God, and this conviction provides him with peace and purpose even in the face of pressure and expectations.

Scheffler's faith also influences the people he surrounds himself with. He met his caddie, Ted Scott, during a Bible study, and their shared Christian beliefs were a big reason for their partnership (Chivers, 2022). Caddie Brad Payne, who subbed for Scott in the 2024 PGA Championship, also shared Scottie's faith.

After winning the Masters, Scottie humbly credited his victory to his faith, explaining that his confidence came from knowing that his ultimate victory had already been secured through Christ's sacrifice.

Scottie's pre-tournament anxieties are well documented, but his reliance on prayer and encouragement from Meredith helped him manage the emotional weight of competition. The morning before the final round at Augusta, for instance, he admitted feeling overwhelmed and unsure of whether he was ready for the challenge. However, after a reassuring conversation with Meredith, who reminded him of his faith and the constancy of God's love regardless of the tournament's outcome, he was able to regain his focus. This type of spiritual grounding has allowed him to remain calm and perform under pressure, eventually securing the green jacket.

For Scottie, golf is simply a means through which to glorify God, and he openly acknowledges that his success is not solely a result of his skills but also of divine providence. He strives to approach every tournament with the mindset that his purpose is to use his talents for a higher calling, and this perspective has allowed him to navigate the highs and lows of his career with grace and humility.

Rocky Hambric: Partner in Business and Faith

Scottie's relationship with his longtime agent, Rocky Hambric, goes beyond just business—it has deep roots in both their professional and personal lives. Rocky met Scottie when he was just eight years old at Royal Oaks Country Club in Dallas, and the bond between the Schefflers and the Hambrics quickly grew stronger. Rocky became an essential mentor in Scottie's life, playing an important part in both his career and his spiritual journey.

As a teenager, when it was time for Scottie's confirmation in the Catholic Church, he chose Rocky as his sponsor (*Labor and Agents: Ties Run Deep between Masters Champ Scottie Scheffler and Golf Agent Rocky Hambric*, 2022). This decision attested to the deep connection between the two families, with both sides considering each other as extended family. Since the Schefflers didn't have any immediate family in Texas due to their New Jersey roots, Hambric became the closest figure to a godfather for Scheffler.

Over the years, Rocky watched as Scottie's golf career flourished, and relished in watching him grow into the world's number-one player. Rocky had seen Scottie's drive and competitiveness from a young age, and this only deepened their connection. The relationship between the two men today symbolizes more than a typical agent-client dynamic; it's a bond based on shared values, faith, and a lifelong friendship.

The Scottie Scheffler and Sam Burns Retreat

Scottie Scheffler and fellow professional golfer Sam Burns have become known for their dedication to mentoring younger players through faith-based events. One such event is the annual retreat they host with the

College Golf Fellowship (CGF), held at the AP Ranch in Fort Worth, Texas. The retreat, which the two golfers sponsor, combines physical activity, fellowship, and spiritual reflection, making it a unique experience for all attendees.

Designed for college golfers, it's a weekend filled with recreational activities such as basketball, pickleball, and even a fun club-throwing competition. In addition to these activities, attendees participate in four Bible study sessions led by CGF staff. These sessions provide an opportunity for golfers to explore how biblical teachings can apply to their lives, both on and off the golf course. Small group discussions follow each session, allowing for deeper reflection and connection with fellow attendees.

The retreat is small, often limited to less than 50 participants. This helps create an intimate environment where the attendees can build meaningful relationships and share their faith journeys. Both Scottie and Sam lead by example during these retreats, showing aspiring Christian golf pros the importance of integrating their faith with their sports careers.

Scottie Goes Full Swing

In 2023, Scottie was prominently featured in *Full Swing*, a Netflix docuseries that provides an in-depth look at life on the PGA Tour, focusing on the highs and lows of professional golfers.

Episode 2 of the series, titled *Win or Go Home*, contrasts Scottie's rapid ascent to becoming the number-one golfer in the world, alongside Brooks Koepka's struggle to regain his form. The show captures Scottie's journey through the 2022 season, showing his grounded and humble personality, often emphasized by his close bond with Meredith. Scottie's impressive victories, including his first Masters win, are highlighted, and viewers see how his calm demeanor and deep faith helped him navigate the pressure of competition.

The docuseries also gives fans a behind-the-scenes view of Scottie's life off the course, offering moments of lightheartedness, and focusing on his balanced approach to life and golf. Unlike Brooks Koepka, who's portrayed as struggling to reconcile his past successes with his recent challenges in the episode, Scottie's presence in the episode offers a glimpse into his gratitude for being on tour and his ability to keep the sport in perspective. If you haven't seen it yet, it's a must-watch!

Other Endeavors

Scottie has expanded his horizons into various sports and business ventures, including emerging athletic fields, lucrative golf endorsements, and significant charitable initiatives.

Pickleball

Scottie has an ownership stake in the Texas Ranchers, a team within Major League Pickleball (MLP). His investment aligns him with other notable Texas athletes who've drummed up enthusiasm about the sport, including Micah Parsons of the Dallas Cowboys and C.J. Stroud of the Houston Texans, who also backed the Ranchers.

Scottie's personal interest in the game stems from its accessibility and broad appeal. He believes that pickleball offers a unique opportunity for fans to engage with the sport on multiple levels—whether by playing it recreationally or by watching professionals compete.

Endorsements

Scottie's rise in the golfing world has not only earned him acclaim; it has also made him one of the wealthiest players on the PGA Tour, with an estimated net worth of around $61 million as of the publishing of this book (Verma, 2024). This rapid accumulation of wealth is attributed to his consistent on-course success, including multiple PGA Tour victories and a historic Masters win, alongside a lucrative portfolio of endorsement deals.

One of Scottie's key endorsement partners is Rolex, a brand synonymous with excellence and precision. After his 2022 Masters win, Scottie was frequently seen wearing the Rolex Submariner "Hulk," a timepiece known for its green bezel and dial, a perfect match for the green jacket of the Masters champion. His association with Rolex reflects his status as a top-tier athlete in the golf world, and his ambassador role with the brand places him alongside legendary figures in the sport.

Scottie's partnership with major sports brands is equally revealing of his standing in the sports world. He wears Nike apparel and footwear during tournaments, and his choice of Nike Tiger Woods Edition shoes in high-stakes events reflects the influence of other golfing greats on his career. In terms of clubs and other equipment, Scheffler signed a deal with TaylorMade in 2022, using their clubs and balls on the course.

In addition to these high-profile deals, Scheffler is an ambassador for Veritex Bank, a partnership that reflects his deep connection to his Texas roots. As a Dallas native, aligning with a local bank reinforces his commitment to his community and values. Through this partnership, Scottie represents the bank's vision of growth and success, both in his sport and within the world of finance.

Philanthropy

Scottie has made a lasting impact on junior golf, particularly through his involvement with the Northern Texas PGA (NTPGA) Foundation. As a former junior golfer himself, having participated in the NTPGA Junior Tour from 2002 to 2010, Scottie holds a deep connection to the organization that helped shape his early career. Reflecting on his time playing junior golf, he credits the NTPGA for helping him develop the skills and passion that would later propel him to success on the PGA Tour.

In 2019, Scottie took his commitment to junior golf further by donating $50,000 of the $300,000 he won through the RSM Birdies Fore Love program to the NTPGA Foundation (NTPGA, 2020). This donation was directed toward the foundation's junior golf and education programs.

Scottie's generous contribution enabled the launch of the Scottie Scheffler/RSM Birdies Fore Love grant program, which provides financial assistance to young golfers who may not have the means to participate in the NTPGA Junior Tour. This initiative covers membership fees and tournament entry costs, ensuring that talented players from all backgrounds can access the same opportunities Scottie had as a junior. Additionally, the grant provides free entry to a first-time Prep Tour event for new junior golfers, promoting the sport's growth at the grassroots level.

Scottie's donation also supported the foundation's educational pillar, with the Scottie Scheffler/RSM Birdies Fore Love Scholarships awarded to college-bound high school seniors. His generous contribution has helped drive athletic and academic development among young players, ensuring his legacy will continue to impact junior golfers for years to come.

The Triumph Over Kid Cancer Foundation

Scottie has also been involved with the Triumph Over Kid Cancer (TOKC) Foundation, an organization that's very close to his heart. His relationship with TOKC began through a personal connection with James Ragan, a young golfer and co-founder of the foundation, who was battling pediatric bone cancer. Scheffler and Ragan first met during their participation in junior golf tournaments, forming a bond that would last throughout Ragan's fight with the disease.

James Ragan passed away in 2014, but his legacy lives on through the TOKC Foundation, which aims to raise awareness and fund research for pediatric cancer. To this day, Scottie is deeply impacted by James' courage and positivity and continues to support the foundation's mission, using his platform to honor his late friend. Scottie has participated in several TOKC fundraising events, including a memorable tournament where he raised money for pediatric cancer research.

Scottie's advocacy for TOKC goes beyond financial support—he carries forward the lessons he learned from Ragan, particularly the importance of living in the moment and appreciating life's blessings. This partnership reflects Scottie's commitment to making a tangible difference in the lives of children battling cancer, and his ongoing efforts with TOKC exemplify the golfer's dedication to using his success for a greater cause.

Don't Forget!

- Baby Bennett joined the Scheffler squad in May 2024, right after Scottie secured his second Masters win.
- Scottie's unwavering Catholic faith shapes his life and career, reminding him it's not all about golf scores—his real win was secured on the cross.

- Yes, it's true! Scottie is now into pickleball too! He's backed the Texas Ranchers and is making moves off the golf course to promote the popular sport.
- Scottie's endorsement game is strong, with top-tier partnerships that include Rolex, Nike, and TaylorMade.
- Scottie's donation to junior golf and his work with Triumph Over Kid Cancer show he's a star off the course too.
- Don't forget to catch Scottie in Netflix's *Full Swing* series, where he shines both as a world-class golfer and a humble, faith-driven family man.

Did You Know?

- Many wonder what Scottie's favorite golf course is. According to him, it's Southern Hills Country Club in Tulsa, Oklahoma.
- And his favorite athlete? Well, it's not a golfer, it's Michael Jordan! When Scottie was a kid, he loved Yankees slugger Derek Jeter.

Time to Pack It in!

Scottie's story shows us how faith, family, and a grounded perspective can guide today's golfers both on and off the golf course. His journey, from early junior golf days to becoming a top PGA Tour player and now a father, is shaped by a sense of purpose that transcends the sport. Scheffler's commitments to philanthropy, business ventures like pickleball, and his deep-rooted beliefs showcase a life well-rounded beyond just golf victories.

But alas, as all good things must come to an end, it's time to haul our clubs back to the caddie shack. The sun's setting, and unless you've got a flashlight to hit those last-minute putts like Scottie used to do with his dad, it's probably time to head home!

Conclusion

As we come to the close of this book, one thing becomes abundantly clear: Scottie Scheffler's story isn't just about mastering a game; it's about mastering life. Through faith, perseverance, and an unyielding sense of purpose, Scottie has shown us what it means to push through life's toughest challenges with grace.

One of Scottie's most telling quotes encapsulates this mindset perfectly: "I can hold my head high... I did my best out there today and fought hard" (The Associated Press, 2023a). Scottie shows us that it's not about winning every time—it's about giving everything you've got, leaving nothing on the table, and walking away knowing you gave your best effort.

At its core, Scottie's story isn't just one of golf excellence, it's a story of resilience and character. He teaches us that setbacks, whether on the golf course or in life, are opportunities to grow and become stronger. Each chapter of his life reflects his unwavering commitment to the values that have shaped him—his family, faith, and community.

There's something incredibly empowering in knowing that success isn't just about how you finish, but how you fight along the way. Whether it's handling the pressure of competing at the Masters or navigating the responsibilities of being a dad to baby Bennett, Scottie has faced each challenge with humility and determination. And in doing so, he's taught us that we too can rise above whatever obstacles life throws at us, so long as we remain steadfast in our goals and refuse to quit.

Scottie's story also brings us back to the power of purpose. Through his faith and the example set by his family, he's consistently shown that life's true fulfillment doesn't come from winning tournaments or amassing wealth. It comes from living with intention—whether that's using his platform to inspire others, giving back to the community, or cherishing the small moments with his loved ones.

As you turn the final page, let Scottie's words and example fuel your own journey. In golf, as in life, not every day will be a victory. You too will have moments of doubt, failure, and frustration. We all do. But never forget that if you give it your all, just as Scottie has done, you can always hold your head high. You'll know that, win or lose, you've fought hard, stayed true to your values, and lived with purpose.

So, whether your own pursuit is in sports, business, or any other part of life, remember Scottie's journey as a beacon of hope and motivation. His story shows us that success isn't just measured in titles or accolades; it's measured in how we show up every day, face adversity, and keep striving toward our goals. Like Scottie, we too can live with the confidence that, as long as we give our best, we can achieve greatness—not just in our careers, but in every aspect of life.

Now, with the lessons of hard work, faith, and resilience fresh in our minds, it's time to close this chapter. As the sun sets on the golf course of life, we may not always hit a perfect shot, but that's okay. The key is to keep swinging, keep pushing, and keep believing. If you do that, you'll find that success—just like Scottie's—isn't about the score but about the strength of your heart and spirit.

And so, as we haul our clubs away and the light fades, unless you've got a flashlight to keep putting, it's time to head home. But remember, the journey continues, and tomorrow, we'll step back onto life's great golf course with renewed determination. Because, just like Scottie, we know that with faith and effort, the next shot could be our best yet.

REFERENCES

Abe, A. (2024, April 15). *Who are Scottie Scheffler's sisters? Meet Molly and Sara who ensured Meredith's absence never affected the champ.* EssentiallySports. https://www.essentiallysports.com/golf-news-pga-tour-who-are-scottie-scheffler-s-sisters-meet-molly-and-sara-who-ensured-merediths-absence-never-affected-the-champ-masters/

Adams, J. (2024a, April 14). *Scottie Scheffler's family paved way for Masters as golfer gets candid.* Heavy. https://heavy.com/sports/golf/scottie-scheffler-family-parents-dad-mom/

Adams, J. (2024b, May 18). *Scottie scheffler's new caddie Brad Payne a nod to faith in PGA championship.* Heavy.com. https://heavy.com/sports/golf/scottie-scheffler-caddie-religion-what-happened/

Adams, M. (2021, September 23). *Scottie Scheffler's PGA coach Randy Smith is a guru of the game.* PGA of America. https://www.pga.com/story/scottie-schefflers-pga-coach-randy-smith-is-a-guru-of-the-game

Agrawal, M. (2023, August 26). *Where did Scottie Scheffler go to college? Exploring the golfer's alma mater.* Sportskeeda. https://www.sportskeeda.com/golf/where-scottie-scheffler-go-college-exploring-golfer-s-alma-mater

Alamg. (2024, May 17). *From Plastic Clubs to Masters Champion: The Childhood of Scottie Scheffler - Kids' Childhood.* Kids' Childhood. https://kidschildhood.com/childhood-of-scottie-scheffler/

Andres, P. (2024, April 14). *Scottie Scheffler sticking to plan for final masters round if wife goes into labor.* Sports Illustrated. https://www.si.com/golf/2024/04/13/scottie-scheffler-sticking-plan-final-masters-round-wife-labor

Angelo. (2024, June 17). *US Open: Scottie Scheffler will reconsider his plans for 2025 after a difficult week - Bondiewithlove.* Bondiewithlove. https://cargreen.es/2024/06/17/bl-wlv/rtsd343878ltcu53uihtml/us-open-scottie-scheffler-will-reconsider-his-plans-for-2025-after-a-difficult-week

The Associated Press. (2020, January 18). *Scottie Scheffler, Andrew Landry enter final round tied at The American Express.* PGA Tour. https://www.pgatour.com/article/news/daily-wrapup/2020/01/18/scottie-scheffler-andrew-landry-share-lead-round-3-the-american-express

The Associated Press. (2022a, February 14). *Scottie Scheffler wins WM Phoenix open for first tour victory.* PGA Tour. https://www.pgatour.com/article/news/daily-wrapup/2022/02/13/scottie-scheffler-wins-wm-phoenix-open-for-first-tour-victory

The Associated Press. (2022b, March 27). *Scottie Scheffler wins WGC-Dell Technologies match play.* PGA Tour. https://www.pgatour.com/article/news/daily-wrapup/2022/03/27/scottie-scheffler-wins-2022-wgc-dell-technologies-match-play

The Associated Press. (2022c, May 29). *Sam Burns beats Scottie Scheffler in playoff to win Charles Schwab Challenge.* PGA Tour. https://www.pgatour.com/article/news/daily-wrapup/2022/05/29/sam-burns-beats-scottie-scheffler-playoff-wins-2022-charles-schwab-challenge

The Associated Press. (2020, August 24). *Scottie Scheffler finishes fourth in Northern Trust after exceptional Friday performance.* Dallas News. https://www.dallasnews.com/sports/golf/2020/08/23/scottie-scheffler-finishes-fourth-in-northern-trust-after-exceptional-friday-performance/

The Associated Press. (2023a, February 12). *Golf roundup: Scottie Scheffler repeats in Phoenix, rises to No. 1 in world again.* Chattanooga Times Free Press. https://www.timesfreepress.com/news/2023/feb/12/golf-roundup-scottie-scheffler-repeats-in-phoenix/

The Associated Press. (2023b, March 13). *Scottie Scheffler back at No.1 after winning The Players.* The Dallas Morning News. https://www.dallasnews.com/sports/golf/2023/03/12/dallas-scottie-scheffler-back-at-no1-after-turning-in-masterpiece-to-win-the-players/

The Associated Press. (2023c, August 18). *Viktor Hovland sets course record with 61 to win BMW Championship - ESPN.* ESPN. https://www.espn.ph/golf/story/_/id/38230006/victor-hovland-sets-course-record-61-win-bmw-championship

The Associated Press. (2023d, December 4). *Golf roundup: Scottie Scheffler's putting progress shows in victory.* Times Free Press. https://www.timesfreepress.com/news/2023/dec/03/golf-roundup-scottie-schefflers-putting-progress/

The Associated Press. (2024a, May 26). *Davis Riley captures first individual tour win by five-stroke margin at Charles Schwab challenge.* PGA Tour. https://www.pgatour.com/article/news/daily-wrapup/2024/05/26/davis-riley-wins-charles-schwab-championship-colonial-country-club-keegan-bradley-scottie-scheffler

The Associated Press. (2024b, May 26). *Davis Riley cruises past Scottie Scheffler to win Charles Schwab challenge.* NBC Sports. https://www.nbcsports.com/golf/news/davis-riley-cruises-past-scottie-scheffler-to-win-charles-schwab-challenge

The Associated Press (2023c, Feb 12). *Recaps (final round): Scottie Scheffler wins the 2023 WM phoenix open - full recap.* CBS Sports. https://www.cbssports.com/golf/leaderboard/pga-tour/28938116/wm-phoenix-open/recap/

The Associated Press. (2024c, June 9). *Scheffler wins Memorial for 5th victory of year; Strom overcomes 7-shot deficit on LPGA Tour.* AP News. https://apnews.com/sports/golf-compensation-in-sports-scott-scheffler-linnea-strom-eb6c4dd20a1c74c9eed547c51d9c323c

The Associated Press. (2024d, June 23). *Scottie Scheffler defeats Tom Kim in playoff at Travelers for sixth victory of season.* PGA Tour. https://www.pgatour.com/article/news/daily-wrapup/2024/06/23/scottie-scheffler-wins-travelers-championship-playoff-tom-kim-sunday-round-4-tpc-river-highlands-weather-cromwell

Audilet, M. (2024, May 25). *Scottie Scheffler's college GPA made headlines.* Athlon Sports. https://athlonsports.com/golf/scottie-schefflers-college-gpa-made-headlines

Badenhausen, K. (2024, June 10). *Scottie Scheffler prize money hits PGA record $24M ahead of U.S. open.* Sportico. https://www.sportico.com/leagues/golf/2024/scottie-scheffler-prize-money-2024-pga-tour-record-1234783575/

Bantock, J. (2022, May 30). *Sam Burns sinks 38-foot putt to defeat "best friend" Scottie Scheffler in Charles Schwab challenge playoff.* CNN. https://edition.cnn.com/2022/05/30/golf/sam-burns-scottie-scheffler-charles-schwab-spt-spc-intl/index.html

Bantock, J. (2023, September 30). *USA's Scottie Scheffler in tears after record Ryder Cup loss, as Europe extend dominance.* CNN. https://edition.cnn.com/2023/09/30/sport/scottie-scheffler-tears-ryder-cup-loss-spt-intl/index.html

Bantock, J. (2024, May 17). *Scottie Scheffler: The new father and man of faith with the golfing world at his feet.* CNN. https://edition.cnn.com/2024/05/17/sport/scottie-scheffler-profile-pga-championship-spt-intl/index.html

Bay, A. (2023, October 9). *25 intriguing facts about Scottie Scheffler.* Facts.net. https://facts.net/celebrity/25-intriguing-facts-about-scottie-scheffler/

Beall, J. (2022, September 24). *Presidents Cup 2022: Scottie Scheffler hit a shank off the face of the Earth.* Golf Digest. https://www.golfdigest.com/story/scheffler-shank-presidents-cup-2022

Beall, J. (2024, May 17). *PGA Championship 2024: Scottie Scheffler arrested and charged with felony by Louisville police following Friday incident at Valhalla.* Golf Digest. https://www.golfdigest.com/story/scottie-scheffler-pga-championship-detained-police-2024

Bell, S. (2016, June 16). *Highland park grad, Texas student Scottie Scheffler the US open clubhouse leader after rain-shortened day 1.* Dallas News. https://www.dallasnews.com/sports/golf/2016/06/16/highland-park-grad-texas-student-scottie-scheffler-the-us-open-clubhouse-leader-after-rain-shortened-day-1/

Benson, P. (2024, May 17). *Scottie Scheffler wears Tiger Woods' Nike shoes in PGA championship.* Kicks on SI; Sports Illustrated. https://www.si.com/fannation/sneakers/news/scottie-scheffler-wears-tiger-woods-nike-shoes-in-pga-championship

Bose, R. (2024, April 12). *World no. 1 golfer Scottie Scheffler's net worth, endorsements and remarkable rise to the top.* Prestige. https://www.prestigeonline.com/hk/leisure/golf/scottie-scheffler-net-worth-endorsements-golf-career/

Brauner, M. (2024, April 15). *Scottie Scheffler shares message of faith after Masters victory – "My victory's secure on the cross."* Yellowhammer News. https://yellowhammernews.com/scottie-scheffler-shares-message-of-faith-after-masters-victory-my-victorys-secure-on-the-cross/

Bull, A. (2024, April 15). Scheffler's superpower ability to let things go was key to Masters romp. *The Guardian.* https://www.theguardian.com/sport/2024/apr/15/scottie-scheffler-superpower-ability-to-let-things-go-was-key-to-masters-romp-golf

By the numbers: Statistics confirm Scottie Scheffler's historical dominance. (n.d.). PGA Tour. https://www.pgatour.com/article/news/latest/2024/04/22/by-the-numbers-scottie-schefflers-historical-dominance-rbc-heritage-masters-the-players-championship-arnold-palmer-invitational

By the numbers: Statistics confirm Scottie Scheffler's historical dominance - PGA TOUR. (n.d.). PGA Tour. https://www.pgatour.com/article/news/latest/2024/04/22/by-the-numbers-scottie-schefflers-historical-dominance-rbc-heritage-masters-the-players-championship-arnold-palmer-invitational

Cameron Champ shoots 69, finds top 10 at U.S. open. (2017). AmateurGolf.com. https://www.amateurgolf.com/golf-tournament-news/19461/Cameron-Champ-shoots-69--finds-top-10-at-U-S--Open

Cannizzaro, M. (2024, June 17). *Scottie Scheffler willing to alter preparation plans after disappointing US Open.* New York Post. https://nypost.com/2024/06/16/sports/scottie-scheffler-willing-to-alter-preparation-after-us-open-disappointment/

Casey, P. (2024a, April 10). *Scottie Scheffler "not going to expand" on secrets of Masters success.* Independent. https://www.independent.co.uk/sport/golf/scottie-scheffler-tiger-woods-augusta-national-augusta-phil-casey-b2526294.html

Casey, P. (2024b, May 12). *Scottie Scheffler reveals plans for caddie missing third round of PGA Championship.* Independent. https://www.independent.co.uk/sport/golf/scottie-scheffler-pga-championship-caddie-b2545421.html

Chicago Tribune. (2019, May 26). *Rising star Scottie Scheffler wins the Evans scholars invitational at the Glen Club in a playoff after a closing 63.* Chicago Tribune. https://www.chicagotribune.com/2019/05/26/rising-star-scottie-scheffler-wins-the-evans-scholars-invitational-at-the-glen-club-in-a-playoff-after-a-closing-63/

Chivers, M. (2022, February 16). *Scottie Scheffler and Ted Scott: A PGA Tour duo made in heaven?* Golfmagic. https://www.golfmagic.com/pga-tour/scottie-scheffler-and-ted-scott-pga-tour-duo-made-heaven

Cohen, J. (2024, May 24). *The University of Texas at . . . California?* Texas Monthly. https://www.texasmonthly.com/arts-entertainment/why-is-texas-hosting-ncaa-golf-championships-in-california/

Cunningham, K. (2024, August 4). *Scottie Scheffler steals Olympic gold medal with epic comeback in Paris.* Golf. https://golf.com/news/scottie-scheffler-wins-olympic-gold-medal-comeback/

Dallas, K. (2024a, April 10). *Scottie Scheffler is the top golfer in the world. He says faith is his defining trait.* Deseret News. https://www.deseret.com/sports/2024/04/09/scottie-scheffler-talks-faith-before-2024-masters/

Dallas, K. (2024b, April 15). *Scottie Scheffler shares his excitement to become a father after second Masters win.* Deseret News. https://www.deseret.com/sports/2024/04/14/scottie-scheffler-dad-after-masters-win/

Davison, D. (2019, October 6). UT-ex Scottie Scheffler is one of golf's budding stars. *Fort Worth Star-Telegram.*

Dethier, D. (2024, August 15). *The 2025 PGA Tour schedule dropped. Here's what's changing (and what it means for LIV).* Golf.com. https://golf.com/news/2025-pga-tour-schedule-dropped-changes-liv/

Dimengo, N. (2024, June 12). *The secrets behind Scottie Scheffler's dominance? He's happy to share.* Golf. https://golf.com/instruction/secrets-scottie-scheffler-dominance-us-open/

Douglas, K. (2024, April 22). *Scheffler claims RBC Heritage for 4th win in last 5 starts.* The Score. https://www.thescore.com/pga/news/2898483

Duca, R. (2012, July 18). *Texan Scheffler finds vagaries of match play in defeat.* USGA. https://www.usga.org/articles/2012/07/going-low-nothing-unusual-for-young-texan-21474848889.html

Durrett, R. (2014a, May 8). *Scheffler set for PGA Tour debut at HP Byron Nelson Championship.* ESPN. https://www.espn.com/dallas/golf/story/_/id/10902321/scheffler-set-pga-tour-debut-hp-byron-nelson-championship-golf

Durrett, R. (2014b, May 18). *Scottie Scheffler, 17, doesn't disappoint at HP Byron Nelson Championship -- golf - ESPN*. ESPN. https://www.espn.com/golf/story/_/id/10950419/scottie-scheffler-17-disappoint-hp-byron-nelson-championship-golf

E. Michael Johnson. (2022, March 27). *The clubs Scottie Scheffler used to win the 2022 WGC-Dell match play*. Golf Digest. https://www.golfdigest.com/story/scottie-scheffler-clubs-used-to-win-2022-wgc-dell-technologies-match-play

Erin. (2017, June 17). *U.S. oper championship 2017 June 17, 2017 Scottie Scheffler*. Asapsports.com. https://www.asapsports.com/show_interview.php?id=131122

Esse, M. (2022, March 9). *Team TaylorMade welcomes Scottie Scheffler*. Taylormade Golf Europe. https://www.taylormadegolf.eu/clubhouse/288811-team-taylormade-welcomes-scottie-scheffler.html?lang=en_ES

Fenner, J. (2024, April 23). *Scottie Scheffler's humble Texas home: Golf's World No 1. lives in $2m, five bedroom Dallas mansion.*. Daily Mail Online. https://www.dailymail.co.uk/sport/golf/article-13340447/Scottie-Schefflers-humble-Texas-home-Golfs-World-No-1-lives-2m-five-bedroom-Dallas-mansion-wife-Meredith-welcome-child-stars-stunning-Masters-RBC-Heritage-triumphs.html

Ferguson, D. (2024a). *Scottie Scheffler unstoppable and wins another Masters green jacket*. Durango Herald. https://www.durangoherald.com/articles/scottie-scheffler-unstoppable-and-wins-another-masters-green-jacket-2/

Ferguson, D. (2024b, March 10). *Scottie Scheffler, with hot putter, demolishes the field to win at Bay Hill*. AP News. https://apnews.com/article/scottie-scheffler-arnold-palmer-invitational-bay-hill-4d5f73925e2464e4aba6c874da59a4f8

Five things to know: Abrdn Scottish Open 2021. (2021, July 7). European Tour. https://www.europeantour.com/g4d-tour/news/articles/detail/five-things-to-know-abrdn-scottish-open-2021/

Fleming, B. (2024, May 18). *PGA Championship 2024: Xander Schauffele leads after Scottie Scheffler plays on despite arrest*. Yahoo Sports. https://uk.sports.yahoo.com/news/scottie-scheffler-detained-police-pga-111339006.html?

Former Longhorn Scheffler wins the memorial tournament. (2024). Southeastern Conference. https://www.secsports.com/news/2024/06/former-longhorn-scheffler-wins-the-memorial-tournament

Four-Peat complete, Texas wins big 12 men's golf title. (2016, May). Big12sports. https://big12sports.com/news/2016/5/1/210926929.aspx

Foust, M. (2019). *Gold medalist Scottie Scheffler says his faith is what defines him the most*. AM 1100 KFAX. https://kfax.com/articles/contributors/michael-foust/gold-medalist-scottie-scheffler-says-his-faith-is-what-defines-him-the-most

Full Swing. (2023, February 15). Netflix. https://www.netflix.com/ph-en/title/81483353

"Full swing" recaps: Episode 2 win or go home. (2023, February 15). PGA Tour. https://www.pgatour.com/article/news/netflix/episode/full-swing-recaps-episode-2-win-or-go-home-scottie-scheffler

Golf Ambassadors. (n.d.). Veritex Community Bank. https://veritexbank.com/about-us/golf-ambassadors/

Golf champion Scottie Scheffler reveals how faith reshaped his soul. (2024, April 24). Good Gospel Playlist. https://goodgospelplaylist.com/golf-champion-scottie-scheffler-reveals-how-faith-reshaped-his-soul/

Golf rules: How to play golf. (2022). Rules of Sport. https://www.rulesofsport.com/sports/golf.html#google_vignette

Golf: Scottie Scheffler wins playoff at Phoenix Open for first PGA Tour win. (2022, February 14). The Straits Times. https://www.straitstimes.com/sport/golf/golf-scottie-scheffler-wins-playoff-at-phoenix-open-for-first-pga-tour-win

Gomes, M. (2024a, July 6). *Scottie Scheffler: Meet the athlete.* NBC Olympics. https://www.nbcolympics.com/news/scottie-scheffler-meet-athlete

Gomes, M. (2024b, July 10). *Scottie Scheffler: Career highlights.* NBC Olympics. https://www.nbcolympics.com/news/scottie-scheffler-career-highlights

Graves, W. (2022, April 11). *A true NJ family affair: Inside Scott Scheffler's journey to his Masters victory.* North Jersey Media Group. https://www.northjersey.com/story/sports/golf/2022/04/11/scott-scheffler-masters-champion-ridgewood-nj/7274981001/

Gurley, A. (2024, April 15). *All About Scottie Scheffler's Parents, Scott and Diane Scheffler.* People. https://people.com/all-about-scottie-scheffler-parents-7975415

Hall, M., & Heath, E. (2021, June 14). *10 big names to have won the US open low amateur honors.* Golf Monthly Magazine. https://www.golfmonthly.com/tour/us-open-low-amateurs

Hartov, O. (2024, April 15). *Masters winner Scottie Scheffler matched his Rolex to his green jacket.* GQ. https://www.gq.com/story/scottie-scheffler-masters-winner-rolex-submariner-hulk

Hawkins, S. (2022, May 29). *Burns playoff birdie to beat No. 1 Scheffler at Colonial.* Associated Press. https://apnews.com/article/sports-sam-burns-nick-price-texas-the-masters-d3d0abdad78ed671ae4d36a1d83d63a9

Haworth, J. (2024, May 18). *Star golfer Scottie Scheffler arrested prior to start of PGA Championship's 2nd round: Report.* ABC News. https://abcnews.go.com/US/number-1-golfer-world-scottie-scheffler-arrested-prior/story?id=110333394

Hearon, S. (2024, August 4). *Scottie Scheffler, wife Meredith Scheffler's relationship timeline.* Us Weekly. https://www.usmagazine.com/celebrity-news/pictures/scottie-scheffler-wife-meredith-schefflers-relationship-timeline/

Hennessey, S. (2024, May 17). *15 things you might not know about Scottie Scheffler.* Golf Digest. https://www.golfdigest.com/story/scottie-scheffler-things-to-know/

Herrington, R. (2016, June 16). *The NBA finals inspired Scottie Scheffler to shoot his opening-round 69 at Oakmont.* Golf Digest. https://www.golfdigest.com/story/the-nba-finals-inspired-scottie-scheffler-to-shoot-his-opening-round-69-at-oakmont

Hirsh, J. (2024, March 10). *Scottie Scheffler (finally!) rides hot putter to Arnold Palmer Invitational title.* Golf.com. https://golf.com/news/scottie-scheffler-wins-arnold-palmer/

Hodowanic, P. (2023, May 14). *On Mother's Day, Scottie Scheffler has more than one reason to say thank you - PGA TOUR.* PGA Tour. https://www.pgatour.com/article/news/latest/2023/05/13/scottie-scheffler-has-more-than-one-reason-to-say-thank-you-on-mothers-day-att-byron-nelson

Jacob, M. K. (2024, April 19). *Exclusive | World's No. 1 golfer Scottie Scheffler purchased a modest $2.1M newlywed home.* New York Post. https://nypost.com/2024/04/19/real-estate/inside-scottie-schefflers-2-1m-texas-home/

Johnson, D. (2020). *Dustin Johnson named 2020 PGA tour player of the year, Scottie Scheffler earns top rookie honors.* CBS Sports. https://www.cbssports.com/golf/news/dustin-johnson-named-2020-pga-tour-player-of-the-year-scottie-scheffler-earns-top-rookie-honors/

Jourdan, C. (2024, April 19). *Who are the candidates for the 2024 Phil Mickelson award?* Golfweek. https://golfweek.usatoday.com/lists/college-golf-2024-phil-mickelson-award-candidates-freshman-of-the-year/*July 2013 week 30 rankings.* (2023). WAGR. https://www.wagr.com/news/2013/july/week-30

Kazlowski, M. (2019, August 22). *Local links: Former Highland Park, Texas golfer Scottie Scheffler wins opener of Korn Ferry finals.* Dallas News. https://www.dallasnews.com/sports/golf/2019/08/22/local-links-former-highland-park-texas-golfer-scottie-scheffler-wins-opener-of-korn-ferry-finals/

Kazlowski, M. (2023, January 26). *Jordan Spieth, Scottie Scheffler to be featured in Netflix show.* Dallas News; The Dallas Morning News. https://www.dallasnews.com/sports/golf/2023/01/25/local-links-pros-jordan-spieth-scottie-scheffler-to-be-featured-in-netflix-golf-series/

Kelly, T. (2024, June 24). *Scottie Scheffler is 5th golfer to surpass $70 million in all-time PGA tour money.* Golfweek. https://golfweek.usatoday.com/2024/06/24/pga-tour-all-time-money-list-scottie-scheffler-fifth/

Kerley, L. (2022, April 19). *How golfer Scottie Scheffler praised god after master's tournament win.* Religion Unplugged. https://religionunplugged.com/news/2022/4/14/analysis-how-golfer-scottie-scheffler-praised-his-god-after-masters-win

Khambe Huda Imran. (2024, April 18). *Scottie scheffler to sacrifice career after fatherhood? 2x masters winner's surprise future plans explored.* EssentiallySports. https://www.essentiallysports.com/golf-news-scottie-scheffler-to-sacrifice-career-after-fatherhood-two-x-masters-winners-surprise-future-plans-explored-pga-tour/

Klatt, R. (2023). *Scheffler winner of Phil Mickelson outstanding freshman award presented by the Phil and Amy Mickelson foundation.* GCAA. https://collegiategolf.com/news/386-scheffler-winner-of-phil-mickelson-outstanding-freshman-award-presented-by-the-phil-and-amy-mickelson-foundation

Krishna, L. (2024, April 22). *WATCH: Scottie Scheffler's parents celebrate 2024 RBC Heritage victory in wholesome moment.* Sportskeeda. https://www.sportskeeda.com/golf/news-watch-scottie-scheffler-s-parents-celebrate-2024-rbc-heritage-victory-wholesome-moment

Labor and Agents: Ties run deep between Masters champ Scottie Scheffler and golf agent Rocky Hambric. (2022, April 18) Sports Business Journal. https://www.sportsbusinessjournal.com/Journal/Issues/2022/04/18/Insiders/Labor-and-Agents.aspx

Landry, A. (2020). *2020 American Express scores: Andrew Landry, Scottie Scheffler break away in desert in Round 3.* CBS Sports. https://www.cbssports.com/golf/news/2020-american-express-scores-andrew-landry-scottie-scheffler-break-away-in-desert-in-round-3/

Larsen, B. (2014, April 26). *Junior Invitational: Scheffler tops Champ.* AmateurGolf.com. https://www.amateurgolf.com/golf-tournament-news/12150/Junior-Invitational--Scheffler-tops-Champ

Leighfield, J., & Easdale, R. (2022, March 20). *Who Is Scottie Scheffler's caddie?* Golf Monthly Magazine. https://www.golfmonthly.com/features/the-game/scottie-schefflers-caddie-212813

Leonard, T. (2023, March 12). *Players 2023: Scottie Scheffler returns to World No. 1 with closing 69 and stunning five-shot victory.* Golf Digest. https://www.golfdigest.com/story/Players2023-scottie-scheffler-wins-championship-by-five-shots-world-number-one

Livie, A. (2022, September 10). *Scottie Scheffler named 2022 PGA tour player of the year, beating rory mcilroy and cameron smith to award.* Eurosport. https://www.eurosport.com/golf/scottie-scheffler-named-2022-pga-tour-player-of-the-year-beating-rory-mcilroy-and-cameron-smith-to-a_sto9137513/story.shtml

Maese, R. (2024, July 16). Scottie Scheffler is good at golf because Scottie Scheffler is good at everything The world's top-ranked golfer is an all-around athlete, which he demonstrated as an "effortless" high school basketball player. *The Washington Post.*

Martin, S. (n.d.). *Scottie Scheffler solves greens, wins Arnold Palmer Invitational by five strokes.* PGA Tour. https://www.pgatour.com/article/news/latest/2024/03/10/scottie-scheffler-solves-greens-wins-arnold-palmer-invitational-by-five-strokes-bay-hill-sean-martin

Martin, S. (2024, May 19). *Scottie Scheffler closes with 65 to wrap wild week at PGA Championship.* PGA Tour. https://www.pgatour.com/article/news/latest/2024/05/19/scottie-scheffler-finishes-with-65-at-2024-pga-championship-top-10-valhalla

Mattura, G. (2022, April 11). *Bergen County golf community takes pride in Scottie Scheffler's Masters win.* North Jersey Media Group. https://www.northjersey.com/story/sports/golf/2022/04/11/bergen-county-golfers-takes-pride-scottie-schefflers-masters-win/7277368001/

McCabe, J. (2016, June 6). *Scottie Scheffler's par save forces tuesday playoff at U.S. open Columbus qualifier.* Golfweek. https://golfweek.usatoday.com/2016/06/06/us-open-sectional-qualifying-scottie-scheffler-columbus-playoff/

McDonald, P. (2024). *Scottie Scheffler arrested while trying to enter Valhalla, released before Round 2 of 2024 PGA Championship.* CBS Sports. https://www.cbssports.com/golf/news/scottie-scheffler-arrested-while-trying-to-enter-valhalla-released-before-round-2-of-2024-pga-championship/

McKnight, J. (2024, May 14). *Scottie Scheffler welcomes baby boy ahead of PGA Championship – adorable first photo.* HELLO! https://www.hellomagazine.com/healthandbeauty/mother-and-baby/553003/scottie-scheffler-welcomes-first-child-baby-boy-ahead-pga-championship/

McLeish, B. (2024, April 15). *Scottie Scheffler wins his second Masters in three years.* ESPN 98.1 FM - 850 AM WRUF. https://www.wruf.com/headlines/2024/04/15/scheffler-wins-masters/

Meet the USA Walker cup team. (2017, August 21). USGA Walker Cup. https://www.usga.org/content/usga/home-page/championships/2017/walker-cup/articles/meet-2017-usa-walker-cup-team.html

Melton, Z. (2022, September 10). *Scottie Scheffler named PGA tour player of year — on college gameday*. Golf.com. https://golf.com/news/scottie-scheffler-pga-tour-poy-gameday/

Melton, Z. (2024). *The keys for easily hitting a draw, according to Scottie Scheffler*. Golf.com. https://golf.com/instruction/scottie-scheffler-keys-hitting-draw-play-smart/

Men's golf's Scheffler named big 12 scholar athlete. (2018, April 18). University of Texas Athletics. https://texaslonghorns.com/news/2018/4/18/mens-golfs-scheffler-named-big-12-scholar-athlete.aspx

Men's golf. (2022). University of Texas Athletics. https://texaslonghorns.com/sports/mens-golf

Meyer, C. (2024, April 14). *Scottie Scheffler Masters history: Best finishes at Augusta national, career majors, wins*. The Augusta Chronicle. https://www.augustachronicle.com/story/sports/pga/2024/04/14/scottie-scheffler-masters-golf-best-finishes-majors-wins-2024-augusta-national/73322039007/

Mike. (2023, April 29). *My favorite golf quotes for kids*. Club and Tee. https://clubandtee.com/golf-quotes-for-kids/

Milko, J. (2023, August 23). *PGA Tour: Scottie Scheffler invests in new pickleball team*. SBNation.com. https://www.sbnation.com/golf/2023/8/23/23842775/pga-news-scottie-scheffler-invest-new-texas-ranchers-pickleball

Milko, J. (2024a, June 13). *After frustrating U.S. Open, Scottie Scheffler to re-consider future plans, 2025 schedule*. MSN. https://www.msn.com/en-us/sports/golf/after-frustrating-u-s-open-scottie-scheffler-to-re-consider-future-plans-2025-schedule/ar-BB1okD70

Milko, J. (2024b, June 16). *U.S. Open: Scottie Scheffler to re-consider 2025 plans after tough week*. SBNation.com. https://www.sbnation.com/golf/2024/6/16/24179706/us-open-scottie-scheffler-re-consider-future-plans-2025

Miller, B. (2024, May 15). The Athletic: Scottie Scheffler's secret: How a "venomous" trash talker became the best golfer in the world. *The New York Times*. https://www.nytimes.com/athletic/5493394/2024/05/15/scottie-scheffler-pga-championship/

Milton, D. (2024, April 15). *Watch spotting: Scottie Scheffler dons the green jacket a second time at the masters wearing a green rolex "hulk" submariner ref. 116610LV*. Hodinkee. https://www.hodinkee.com/articles/scottie-scheffler-wearing-a-green-rolex-hulk

Morning Read Staff. (2021, September 26). *2021 Ryder Cup: Americans win back cup with dominant performance*. Sports Illustrated. https://www.si.com/golf/news/2021-ryder-cup-scores-live-updates-from-whistling-straits

Morse, B. (2022, May 20). *Masters champion and world No. 1 Scottie Scheffler likely to miss PGA Championship cut*. CNN. https://edition.cnn.com/2022/05/20/golf/scottie-scheffler-miss-cut-2022-pga-championship-spt-intl/index.html

Newsham, G. (2023, March 25). *Inside the PGA Tour Bible Study Group helping golf No. 1 Scottie Scheffler*. New York Post. https://nypost.com/2023/03/25/pga-tour-bible-study-group-helps-golfs-scottie-scheffler/

Nicholson, J. (2020, January 19). *Texans Scheffler, Landry lead way*. Austin American-Statesman. https://www.statesman.com/story/sports/pga/2020/01/19/texans-scheffler-landry-lead-way/1872873007/

9 reasons why everyone should play golf. (n.d.). Harbor Hills Club. https://www.harborhillsclub.com/blog/37-9-reasons-why-everyone-should-play-golf

No. 1 men's golf lands three on academic all-big 12 first team. (2016, April 14). University of Texas Athletics. https://texaslonghorns.com/news/2016/4/14/no-1-mens-golf-lands-three-on-academic-all-big-12-first-team.aspx

No. 14 men's golf, Scheffler lead big 12 championship after three rounds. (2017, April 25). University of Texas Athletics. https://texaslonghorns.com/news/2017/4/25/no-14-mens-golf-scheffler-lead-big-12-championship-after-three-rounds

No.1 Scheffler says patience and trust are secrets to success at Augusta. (2024, April 10). Bilyonaryo Business News. https://bilyonaryo.com/2024/04/10/no-1-scheffler-says-patience-and-trust-are-secrets-to-success-at-augusta/golf/

NTPGA. (2020, July). *PGA tour rookie scottie scheffler's donation makes lasting impact on junior golf.* NTPGA Junior Golf. https://www.ntpgajuniorgolf.com/pga-tour-rookie-scottie-scheffler-s-donation-makes-lasting-impact-on-junior-golf

O'Connor, I. (2021, April 7). *Scottie Scheffler has shot to be first New Jersey-born golfer to win Masters.* New York Post. https://nypost.com/2021/04/06/scottie-scheffler-has-shot-to-be-first-new-jersey-born-golf-to-win-masters/

Obrien, J. (2014, May 19). *TOKC supports Scottie Scheffler.* Triumph over Kids Cancer. https://triumphoverkidcancer.org/co-founder-james-a-ragan-and-his-friend-and-tokc-supporter-scottie-scheffler/

Olympics: Scheffler adds Paris golf gold to impressive 2024 season. (2024, August 5). Kyodo News+. https://english.kyodonews.net/news/2024/08/d3f7d165da62-olympics-scheffler-adds-olympic-gold-to-impressive-2024-season.html

1-2-1 Support. (2022). *How Scottie Scheffler can become golf's first $50 million man.* Bodega Harbour Golf. https://www.bodegaharbourgolf.com/no-module-layout/56-how-scottie-scheffler-can-become-golf-s-first-50-million-man

O'Sullivan, B. (2024, May 16). *Scottie Scheffler family tree: Golfer and wife Meredith welcome baby boy in time for PGA Championship.* The Sporting News. https://www.sportingnews.com/us/golf/news/scottie-scheffler-family-tree-wife-baby-pga-championship/52a3f6884accc8db5afc48a1

Pairings set for 2016 big 12 men's golf championship. (2016, April 25). Big12sports. https://big12sports.com/news/2016/4/25/210910915.aspx

Paris Olympics 2024: World No. 1 golfer Scottie Scheffler wins men's golf gold on his debut. (2024, August 5). WION. https://www.wionews.com/videos/paris-olympics-2024-world-no-1-golfer-scottie-scheffler-wins-mens-golf-gold-on-his-debut-747180

People on the Move: Diane Scheffler, Foley Hoag chief operating officer. (n.d.). Crain's. https://www.crainsnewyork.com/people-on-the-move/diane-scheffler

Persac, N. (2015, May 4). *Tower shines May 4 for men's golf big 12 title.* UT News. https://news.utexas.edu/2015/05/04/tower-shines-may-4-for-mens-golf-big-12-title/

Peters, A. (2024). *Scottie Scheffler beats Tom Kim in playoff at travelers championship; 6th win of 2024.* Bleacher Report. https://bleacherreport.com/articles/10125785-scottie-scheffler-beats-tom-kim-in-playoff-at-travelers-championship-6th-win-of-2024

PGA Tour. (2020, August 9). *Tweet: Fun facts about Scottie Scheffler.* X. https://x.com/PGATOUR/status/1292570952677679104

PGA tour blog: On winning the players championship for the first time. (2023, March 16). Philstar Global. https://qa.philstar.com/sports/2023/03/16/2252141/pga-tour-blog-winning-players-championship-first-time

PGA Tour releases dates for Byron Nelson, colonial. (2024, August 15). Dallas News. https://www.dallasnews.com/sports/golf/2024/08/14/golf-byron-nelson-colonial-charles-schwab-tpc-craig-ranch-pga-tour-scottie-scheffler/

Phatak, S. (2023, August 24). *$50,000,000 World No. 1 golfer Scottie Scheffler invests in USA's "fastest growing sport."* Sportskeeda. https://www.sportskeeda.com/golf/news-50-000-000-world-number-1-golfer-scottie-scheffler-invests-usa-s-fastest-growing-sport

Pietruszkiewicz, N. (2023, May 10). *Dream team: Was 2017 USA Walker cup team the best ever?* USGA Walker Cup. https://championships.usga.org/walkercup/2023/articles/dream-team--is-2017-usa-team-best-ever-.html

The Players 2023: Scottie Scheffler. (2023). The Players. https://www.theplayers.com/past-champions/scottie-scheffler-2023

Politi, S. (2022, April 11). *Scottie Scheffler's Masters victory is a great moment for New Jersey sports, too.* NJ.com. https://www.nj.com/sports/2022/04/scottie-schefflers-masters-victory-is-a-great-moment-for-new-jersey-sports-too-politi.html

Politi, S. (2023, April 4). *Tracing a Masters champion's first swings at an unlikely N.J. golf course.* NJ.com. https://www.nj.com/sports/2023/04/tracing-a-masters-champions-first-swings-at-an-unlikely-nj-golf-course-politi.html

Porter, K. (2022a, March 27). *2022 WGC-Dell match play winner, grades: Scottie Scheffler gets third victory of last two months.* CBS Sports. https://www.cbssports.com/golf/news/2022-wgc-dell-match-play-winner-grades-scottie-scheffler-gets-third-victory-of-last-two-months/

Porter, K. (2022b, February 14). *2022 WM Phoenix Open leaderboard, grades: Scottie Scheffler survives three-hole playoff for first PGA Tour win.* CBS Sports. https://www.cbssports.com/golf/news/2022-wm-phoenix-open-leaderboard-grades-scottie-scheffler-survives-three-hole-playoff-for-first-pga-tour-win/live/

Quinn, B. (2024, June 12). The lesson of Scottie Scheffler at this U.S. Open, from the man who taught him. *The Spokesman Review.*

Rahul. (2024, April 15). *Scottie scheffler is half-white and half-italian; what are the odds?!* PopTV Culture. https://poptvculture.com/scottie-scheffler-italian/

Randy Smith. (2024). Texas Golf Hall of Fame. https://www.texasgolfhof.org/exhibit/randy-smith

Richardson, J. (2023, December 20). *Scottie Scheffler's net worth, career earnings and $6m endorsements including Nike and TaylorMade deals.* Golf365. https://www.golf365.com/features/scottie-schefflers-net-worth-career-earnings-and-endorsement-deals-including-nike-and-taylormade-deals

Riddell, D., & Bantock, J. (2024, March 12). *Why Grandma's chocolate pie and staying humble is the perfect recipe for world No. 1 Scottie Scheffler.* CNN. https://edition.cnn.com/2024/03/12/sport/scottie-scheffler-grandma-players-championship-spt-intl/index.html

Ridgewood born Scottie Scheffler becomes first New Jersey golfer to win Masters. (2022, April 10). TAPinto Ridgewood. https://www.tapinto.net/towns/ridgewood/sections/sports/articles/ridgewood-born-scottie-scheffler-becomes-first-new-jersey-golfer-to-win-masters

Rodini, L. (2024, July 9). *Scottie Scheffler's net worth: How much pro golf's #1 player makes in 2024.* The Street. https://www.thestreet.com/sports/scottie-scheffler-net-worth-salary-career

Romine, B. (2017a, April 26). *Texas edges oklahoma state to continue big 12 championship win streak.* Golfweek. https://golfweek.usatoday.com/2017/04/26/big-12-golf-championship-texas-oklahoma-state/

Romine, B. (2017b, May 28). *Scottie Scheffler shows up big for Texas at NCAA championship.* Golfweek. https://golfweek.usatoday.com/2017/05/28/ncaa-golf-men-texas-scottie-scheffler/

Romine, B. (2017c, June 15). *Led by Scottie Scheffler and Cameron Champ, amateurs impress on Day 1 at U.S. open.* Golfweek. https://golfweek.usatoday.com/2017/06/15/us-open-amateurs-day-1-recap-scottie-scheffler-cameron-champ/

Romine, B. (2018, December 10). *Q-School wrap: Walker medals, Xiong second.* NBC Sports; NBC Sports. https://www.nbcsports.com/golf/news/danny-walker-medals-webcom-tour-q-school-norman-xiong-andy-zhang-notch-top-10s

Rookie of Year Scottie Scheffler returns for encore season. (2020, September 30). PGA Tour. https://www.pgatour.com/article/news/latest/2020/09/30/rookie-of-year-scottie-scheffler-returns-for-encore-season-sanderson-farms-championship

RSM birdies fore love extends program through 2025. (2021a). Sports Destinations. https://www.sportsdestinations.com/sports/golf/rsm-birdies-fore-love-extends-program-through-2025-21484

RSM birdies fore love extends program through 2025. (2021b, September 8). RSM Classic PGA TOUR Event. https://rsmclassic.com/rsm-birdies-fore-love-extends-program-through-2025/

Rumsey, D. (2024, May 13). *Tiger, Scottie at golf's next major.* Front Office Sports. https://frontofficesports.com/newsletter/tiger-scottie-at-golfs-next-major/

Ryder Cup: Match recaps, Day 2. (2021, September 25). PGA Tour. https://www.pgatour.com/article/news/latest/2021/09/25/ryder-cup-match-recaps-day-two-whistling-straits

Sakmari, E. (2022, August 24). *Golf's Scottie Scheffler is worth millions but still drives a 2012 yukon his dad gave him.* NBC 5 Dallas-Fort Worth. https://www.nbcdfw.com/news/sports/scottie-scheffler-is-worth-millions-but-still-drives-a-2012-yukon-his-dad-gave-him/3056001/

Scheffler advances to quarters at polo junior. (2014). AmateurGolf. https://www.amateurgolf.com/golf-tournament-news/11433/Scheffler-Advances-to-Quarters-at-Polo-Junior

Scheffler defeats Riley To win U.S. junior amateur. (2013, July 22). USGA. https://www.usga.org/content/usga/home-page/articles/2013/07/scheffler-defeats-riley-to-win-us-junior-amateur-21474858457.html

Scheffler leads Men's Golf in partial NCAA Championship opening round. (2018, May 25). University of Texas Athletics. https://texaslonghorns.com/news/2018/5/25/scheffler-leads-mens-golf-in-partial-ncaa-championship-opening-round.aspx

Scheffler named Rolex junior player of the year. (2013, October 29). AJGA. https://www.ajga.org/news/scheffler-named-rolex-junior-player-of-the-year

Scheffler ties for second, moves to world no. 1. (2023, May 22). PGA Championship . https://www.pgachampionship.com/news-media/articles/scheffler-ties-for-second-moves-to-world-no-1

Scheffler wins Phil Mickelson award. (2015, June 3). University of Texas Athletics. https://texaslonghorns.com/news/2015/6/3/MGOLF_0603154542

Schlabach, M. (2024a, April 14). *Scottie Scheffler closes with 68, wins another Masters title*. ESPN. https://www.espn.ph/golf/story/_/id/39944182/scottie-scheffler-wins-second-masters-final-round-68

Schlabach, M. (2024b, April 15). *Scottie Scheffler wins by 4 shots, captures another Masters*. ABC News. https://abcnews.go.com/Sports/scottie-scheffler-wins-4-shots-captures-masters/story?id=109226729

Schlabach, M., & Uggetti, P. (2024, April 15). *Answering golf's biggest questions after Scottie Scheffler's Masters win*. ESPN. https://www.espn.ph/golf/story/_/id/39945493/masters-2024-scottie-scheffler-win-mean-rory-mcilroy-tiger-woods

Schmitt, T. (2022, May 29). *Sam Burns buries long putt to beat his buddy Scottie Scheffler in a playoff, taking 2022 Charles Schwab challenge title*. Golfweek. https://golfweek.usatoday.com/2022/05/29/sam-burns-takes-charles-schwab-challenge/

Schupak, A. (2022a, February 13). *From dinging a yellow pole as a kid to defeating Patrick Cantlay in three-hole playoff at WM Phoenix Open, Scottie Scheffler has been destined for greatness*. Golfweek. https://golfweek.usatoday.com/2022/02/13/pga-tour-scottie-scheffler-patrick-cantlay-phoenix-open/

Schupak, A. (2022b, February 15). *How Scottie Scheffler convinced Ted Scott to caddie for him and why it paid quick dividends in Phoenix*. Golfweek. https://golfweek.usatoday.com/2022/02/15/scottie-scheffler-ted-scott-wm-phoenix-open/

Schupak, A. (2022c, March 6). *Scottie Scheffler proves he's a fighter with second PGA Tour win in last three starts (this one at Arnold Palmer Invitational)*. Golfweek. https://golfweek.usatoday.com/2022/03/06/scottie-scheffler-wins-arnold-palmer-invitational-bay-hill/

Schupak, A. (2022d, August 21). *Presidents Cup 2022: Meet the six automatic qualifiers for Team USA*. Golfweek. https://golfweek.usatoday.com/lists/presidents-cup-2022-six-automatic-qualifiers-team-usa/

Schupak, A. (2023a, February 12). *Scottie Scheffler defends title at 2023 WM Phoenix open, returns to world No. 1*. Yahoo Sports. https://sports.yahoo.com/scottie-scheffler-defends-title-win-230314061.html

Schupak, A. (2023b, May 10). *How Scottie Scheffler met his agents — when he was 6 — and formed a relationship that "goes beyond business."* Golfweek. https://golfweek.usatoday.com/2023/05/10/scottie-scheffler-top-billing-2023-att-byron-nelson/

Schupak, A. (2024, May 13). *Meredith and Scottie Scheffler welcome their first child to the world*. Golfweek. https://golfweek.usatoday.com/2024/05/13/meredith-scottie-scheffler-welcome-first-child/

Scottie. (2020). Golfposer. https://www.golfposer.com/players/scottie-scheffler

Scottie Scheffler. (n.d.). European Golf Society. https://europeangolfsociety.com/speaker/scottie-scheffler/

Scottie Scheffler. (2024a). PGA Tour. https://www.pgatour.com/player/46046/scottie-scheffler/latest/video

Scottie Scheffler. (2024b). Sportskeeda. https://www.sportskeeda.com/player/scottie-scheffler#scottie-scheffler-0

Scottie Scheffler. (2024c). Olympics. https://olympics.com/en/athletes/scottie-scheffler

Scottie Scheffler. (2024d). PGA Tour. https://www.pgatour.com/korn-ferry-tour/player/46046/scottie-scheffler/career

Scottie Scheffler. (2024e). Masters. https://www.masters.com/en_US/players/player_46046.html

Scottie Scheffler 1st, Tiger Woods 18th at hero world challenge. (2023, December 3). ESPN. https://www.espn.ph/golf/story/_/id/39036637/scottie-scheffler-1st-tiger-woods-18th-hero-world-challenge

Scottie Scheffler and Sam Burns retreat. (2021). CGF. https://www.collegegolffellowship.com/event-details/scottie-scheffler-and-sam-burns-retreat

Scottie Scheffler career hole in ones. (2024). StatMuse. https://www.statmuse.com/pga/ask/scottie-scheffler-career-hole-in-ones

Scottie Scheffler earns 12th PGA tour title at travelers championship, further bolstering No. 1 position in U.S. Team standings. (2024). President's Cup. https://www.presidentscup.com/news/2024/06/24/scheffler-bolsters-no-1-position-in-us-team-standings

Scottie Scheffler golf quotes, mental profile & biography. (2018). Mindtraining.net. https://mindtraining.net/motivational-quotes/sports-champions/scottie-scheffler.php

Scottie Scheffler highlights from the 2017 NCAA golf championships. (2022, April 11). NCAA. https://www.ncaa.com/video/golf-men/2022-04-11/scottie-scheffler-highlights-2017-ncaa-golf-championships

Scottie Scheffler PGA tour latest. (2024). PGA Tour. https://www.pgatour.com/player/46046/scottie-scheffler/latest/video

Scottie Scheffler wins $300,000 for charity through RSM Birdies Fore Love program. (2019). Rsmcanada.com. https://rsmcanada.com/newsroom/2019/scottie-scheffler-wins-300-000-for-charity-through-rsm-birdies-f.html

Scottie scheffler wins $300,000 for charity through RSM birdies fore love program. (2024). Rsmus.com. https://rsmus.com/newsroom/2019/scottie-scheffler-wins-300000-for-charity-through-rsm-birdies-fo.html

Scottie Scheffler wins hero world challenge; Tiger Woods finishes 18th. (2023, December 3). CBC. https://www.cbc.ca/sports/golf/pga-hero-world-challenge-dec-3-1.7047900

Scottie Scheffler wins Jack Nicklaus Award as PGA Tour player of the year. (2022, September 10). PGA Tour. https://www.pgatour.com/article/news/latest/2022/09/10/scottie-scheffler-voted-2022-jack-nicklaus-award-winner-pga-tour-player-of-year

Scottie Scheffler wins Jack Nicklaus Award as PGA Tour player of the year for second consecutive season. (2024, January 3). PGA Tour. https://www.pgatour.com/article/news/latest/2024/01/03/scottie-scheffler-wins-jack-nicklaus-award-as-pga-tour-player-of-the-year-for-second-consecutive-season-eric-cole-rookie-of-the-year

Scottie Scheffler withdraws from 2020 U.S. Open. (2020). USGA Media Center. https://mediacenter.usga.org/press-releases?item=122813

Scottie Scheffler: What's in the bag. (2024). TaylorMade Golf. https://www.taylormadegolf.com/tourplayers/scottie-scheffler.html?lang=en_US

Scottie Scheffler's not so secret weapon. (2024). Christians in Sport. https://christiansinsport.org.uk/resources/scottie-schefflers-not-so-secret-weapon/

The secret behind Scottie Scheffler's sustained success. (2024, April 11). Michael LoRé. https://michael-lore.com/2024/04/11/the-secret-behind-scottie-schefflers-sustained-success/

Shedloski, D. (2023, December 3). *Hero world challenge winner Scottie Scheffler learned a lesson to close out 2023. Here's what it means for 2024.* Golf Digest. https://www.golfdigest.com/story/scottie-scheffler-hero-world-challenge-win-lesson-for-2024

Singh, K. (2023, August 6). *Who are Scottie Scheffler's sisters? Everything you need to know about Callie, Sara, and Mollie Scheffler.* Sportskeeda. https://www.sportskeeda.com/golf/news-who-scottie-scheffler-s-sisters-everything-need-know-callie-sara-mollie-scheffler

SK Desk. (2024a, June 4). *How much money does Scottie Scheffler make on endorsements?* Sportskeeda. https://www.sportskeeda.com/golf/scottie-scheffler-endorsement-earnings

SK Desk. (2024b, June 4). *Scottie Scheffler's Parents.* Sportskeeda. https://www.sportskeeda.com/golf/scottie-scheffler-parents

SK Desk. (2024c, June 4). *What religion is Scottie Scheffler?* Sportskeeda. https://www.sportskeeda.com/golf/scottie-scheffler-religion

SK Desk. (2024d, August 15). *Scottie Scheffler PGA tour wins.* Sportskeeda. https://www.sportskeeda.com/golf/scottie-scheffler-tour-wins

SK Desk. (2024e, August 15). *Scottie Scheffler PGA tour wins.* Sportskeeda. https://www.sportskeeda.com/golf/scottie-scheffler-tour-wins

Staff. (2024, May 14). *Scottie Scheffler, wife Meredith welcome first child ahead of PGA Championship.* PGA Tour. https://www.pgatour.com/article/news/latest/2024/05/13/scottie-scheffler-wife-meredith-welcome-first-child-baby-boy-ahead-of-pga-championship

Stafford, A. (2023, October). *Ryder Cup: Europe regain trophy as Rory McIlroy and Viktor Hovland star in victory over USA in Rome.* Sky Sports. https://www.skysports.com/golf/news/12176/12974152/ryder-cup-europe-regain-trophy-as-rory-mcilroy-and-viktor-hovland-star-in-victory-over-usa-in-rome

Stats Perform. (2024, August 5). *Paris olympics 2024: "I'll remember it for a long time" - emotional Scottie Scheffler revels in gold medal win.* Outlook India. https://www.outlookindia.com/sports/others/paris-olympics-2024-ill-remember-it-for-a-long-time-emotional-scottie-scheffler-revels-in-oly-gold-medal-win

Stroope, R. (2014, March 21). *UIL individual champ back for Highland Park golf team, in state's top two for last 14 years.* Dallas News. https://www.dallasnews.com/news/2014/03/21/uil-individual-champ-back-for-highland-park-golf-team-in-state-s-top-two-for-last-14-years/

Texas. (2014, April 30). *Video: Big 12 Men's Golf Championship final-round highlights [April 27, 2014].* University of Texas Athletics. https://texaslonghorns.com/news/2014/4/30/MGOLF_0430145719

Texas. (2015, April 29). *No. 2 Men's Golf wins third-straight Big 12 championship.* University of Texas Athletics. https://texaslonghorns.com/news/2015/4/29/MGOLF_0429154513.aspx

Texas. (2016, October 31). *Scheffler wins individual title, men's golf seeded No. 2 at East Lake cup.* University of Texas Athletics. https://texaslonghorns.com/news/2016/10/31/scheffler-wins-individual-title-mens-golf-seeded-no-2-at-east-lake-cup.aspx?path=mgolf

Texas. (2017, April 24). *No. 15 men's golf in sixth after round one at big 12 championship.* University of Texas Athletics. https://texaslonghorns.com/news/2017/4/24/no-15-mens-golf-in-sixth-after-round-one-at-big-12-championship

Texas golfer, Highland Park-ex Scottie Scheffler qualifies for U.S. open spot. (2017, June 6). Dallas News. https://www.dallasnews.com/sports/golf/2017/06/06/texas-golfer-highland-park-ex-scottie-scheffler-qualifies-for-u-s-open-spot/

Texas teen Scheffler sets two scoring marks in Dallas. (2012, June 28). USGA. https://www.usga.org/articles/2012/06/texas-teen-scheffler-sets-two-scoring-marks-21474847643.html

theblackprofessor. (2004). *Can someone explain to me why golf is fun?* Reddit. https://www.reddit.com/r/AskReddit/comments/gs7jb/can_someone_explain_to_me_why_golf_is_fun/

Three AJGA juniors claim amateur titles. (2013, July 29). AJGA. https://www.ajga.org/news/three-ajga-juniors-claim-amateur-titles

Townsend, B. (2014a, May 16). *Highland Park prodigy Scottie Scheffler makes cut at Byron Nelson Championship, eyes even more.* Dallas News. https://www.dallasnews.com/sports/golf/2014/05/16/highland-park-prodigy-scottie-scheffler-makes-cut-at-byron-nelson-championship-eyes-even-more/

Townsend, B. (2014b, May 16). *In PGA debut, 17-year-old Dallas phenom Scottie Scheffler rallies late, brings longtime instructor to tears.* Dallas News. https://www.dallasnews.com/sports/golf/2014/05/16/in-pga-debut-17-year-old-dallas-phenom-scottie-scheffler-rallies-late-brings-longtime-instructor-to-tears/

Trainor, D. (2024, June 11). *Scottie scheffler's parents reveal how they found out about their son's shocking arrest.* Yahoo Entertainment. https://www.yahoo.com/entertainment/scottie-scheffler-parents-reveal-found-142534231.html

Tremlett, S., Heath, E., & Leighfield, J. (2023, January 26). *Scottie Scheffler facts: 30 things you didn't know about the two-time major champion.* Golf Monthly Magazine. https://www.golfmonthly.com/tour/scottie-scheffler-facts-bio

Triumph over kid cancer foundation – teeing off on kids cancer with Scottie Scheffler and friends. (2024, March 27). PaperCity Magazine. https://www.papercitymag.com/events/triumph-over-kid-cancer-fountdation-teeing-off-on-kids-cancer-with-scottie-scheffler-and-friends/

2013 Rolex junior all-America teams boys division. (2013, October 29). AJGA. https://www.ajga.org/news/2013-rolex-junior-all-america-teams-boys-division

2017-18 men's golf roster: Scottie Scheffler. (2022). University of Texas Athletics. https://texaslonghorns.com/sports/mens-golf/roster/scottie-scheffler/7516

USA Today Sports. (2022). *Masters 2022: Scottie Scheffler cruises to first green jacket; Tiger Woods shoots 78.* USA Today. https://www.usatoday.com/story/sports/golf/2022/04/10/masters-sunday-final-round-live-updates-scottie-scheffler-tiger-woods/9527425002/

Verma, I. (2024, August 6). *Scottie Scheffler net worth 2024: How much money does he make?* Yahoo Entertainment. https://www.yahoo.com/entertainment/scottie-scheffler-net-worth-2024-070441294.html

Veteran law firm leader Diane Scheffler joins Troutman Sanders as chief operating officer. (2018). Metro Atlanta CEO. https://metroatlantaceo.com/news/2018/07/veteran-law-firm-leader-diane-scheffler-joins-troutman-sanders-chief-operating-officer/

Warnock, C. (2023, April 2). *Scottie Scheffler's family: 5 fast facts you need to know.* Heavy.com; Heavy. https://heavy.com/sports/golf/scottie-scheffler-family/

Watch: Scottie Scheffler competes in the 2017 NCAA golf championships. (2022, April 11). NCAA. https://www.ncaa.com/news/golf-men/article/2022-04-11/watch-scottie-scheffler-competes-2017-ncaa-golf-championships

Who is Scottie Scheffler's wife? All about Meredith Scudder. (n.d.). Peoplemag. https://people.com/sports/who-is-meredith-scudder-scottie-scheffler-wife/

Why is golf fun? (2024). J. Drew Rogers. https://www.jdrewrogers.com/blog/16/why-is-golf-fun

Wildhack, S. (2019, August 18). *Scottie Scheffler wins nationwide children's hospital championship for second Korn Ferry Tour title - PGA TOUR.* Korn Ferry Tour. https://www.pgatour.com/korn-ferry-tour/article/news/daily-wrapup/2019/08/18/scottie-scheffler-wins-nationwide-childrens-hospital-championship-for-second-korn-ferry-tour-title

A winning team for many years, Scheffler siblings reunite at Augusta. (2023). Power Fades. https://www.powerfades.com/features/20278d8b-8bfc-479a-9494-b25eba8db4b6

Woodard, A. (2024, May 19). *Scottie Scheffler planning to play next week on PGA Tour after "hectic" week at 2024 PGA Championship.* Golfweek. https://golfweek.usatoday.com/2024/05/19/scottie-scheffler-arrest-2024-pga-championship-pga-tour/

Yadav, A. (2023, February 13). *Scottie Scheffler defends 2023 WM Phoenix open title, set to return to World No. 1.* Sportskeeda. https://www.sportskeeda.com/golf/news-scottie-scheffler-defends-2023-wm-phoenix-open-title-set-return-world-no-1

Printed in Great Britain
by Amazon